CHRISTIAN PHILOSOPHY AS A WAY OF LIFE

CHRISTIAN PHILOSOPHY AS A WAY OF LIFE

An Invitation to Wonder

ROSS D. INMAN

Baker Academic
a division of Baker Publishing Group
Grand Rapids, Michigan

Published by Baker Academic
a division of Baker Publishing Group
Grand Rapids, Michigan
www.bakeracademic.com

Printed in the United States of America

Library of Congress Cataloging-in-Publication Data
Names: Inman, Ross D., author.
Title: Christian philosophy as a way of life : an invitation to wonder / Ross D. Inman.
Description: Grand Rapids, Michigan : Baker Academic, a division of Baker Publishing Group, [2023] | Includes bibliographical references and index.
Identifiers: LCCN 2023014299 | ISBN 9781540965738 (paperback) | ISBN 9781540966810 (casebound) | ISBN 9781493442799 (ebook) | ISBN 9781493442805 (pdf)
Subjects: LCSH: Philosophy and religion. | Wonder (Philosophy) | Christian life. | Conduct of life—Philosophy.
Classification: LCC BR100 .I4739 2023 | DDC 201/.61—dc23/eng/20230523
LC record available at https://lccn.loc.gov/2023014299

Baker Publishing Group publications use paper produced from sustainable forestry practices and post-consumer waste whenever possible.

23   24   25   26   27   28   29   7   6   5   4   3   2   1

To Hudson, Declan, and Verity:
may you be eternally enthralled
by the Supreme Wisdom and Wonder of it all

Full of wonder then are all things, which we never think to wonder at because . . . we have, by habit, become dull to the consideration of them.

—Gregory the Great, *Moralia in Job* 6.18

CONTENTS

ACKNOWLEDGMENTS

This book would not have been possible without the steady and stable love of my dear wife, Suzanne. She is my treasured companion, my wise counsel, and my earthly anchor who steadies me amid the joys and flux of life on the Way.

I dedicate this book to my three young children: Hudson, Declan, and Verity. How often they have redirected my wayward attention and lifted my downward gaze to the more weighty and wonderful realities at hand. More than any scholarly book, my children have taught me how to see the ordinary and mundane with new eyes and to wonder at the true depths of God's creatures, great and small. They are daily reminders to me that it is those who are humble and simple in heart who are more apt to see "the wonder of it all." I dedicate this book to them in the hope that they will employ every facet of their being in the pursuit of a life of "joy based in the truth," as Augustine put it.

I'd like to thank my dear friends Travis Dickinson, Paul Gould, and Keith Loftin for their thoughtful feedback on a previous draft of the book. I also owe a debt of gratitude to my friend and graduate assistant, Chris Lee, for his keen editorial eye and his help in seeing this book through to completion.

INTRODUCTION

The primary purpose of this book is to help you take a few small steps toward reframing the way you (likely) think about philosophy as a Christian. There are many excellent books designed to introduce you to the core subdisciplines of philosophy (metaphysics, epistemology, ethics, logic) or to survey the landscape of Western philosophy from a Christian perspective. As you will see, this book is very different, by design. It aims to explore the deeper, motivational question of why to bother with philosophy as a Christian in the first place. You might think of it as a primer for the study of philosophy as a Christian.

It is no secret that philosophy has a public relations problem today. This book is my attempt to join philosophy's PR team and do my small part to help bolster its declining public image, pro bono. The philosophical life, broadly construed, is not a hindrance to the human life well lived; it is a vital ingredient of it. It is not a sidetrack to the Christian life and ministry; it is part of their very substance. My hope for you, dear reader, is that after you have finished this book, a claim that once seemed obviously outlandish—the claim that living philosophically as a Christian is one of the most practical ways you can live your life—will seem outlandish no more.

This book is written for Christians who are philosophical novices, those who are coming to the study of philosophy for the very first time. Of course, all authors hope that their intellectual labors will reach beyond their intended primary audience, and I am certainly no exception. I hope that philosophical veterans—my fellow Christian philosophers who labor together in the academic guild—will also consider the value of recovering a vision of Christian philosophy as a way of life more broadly.

Let me briefly lay out the trajectory of the book as a whole. Chapter 1 explores the distinctively human experience of wonder, what our best psychological science tells us it is and how it is good for us individually and collectively. Chapter 2 then takes up the long-standing view in Western philosophy that wonder is the very lifeblood—the beginning, middle, and end—of the philosophical life. Though the connection between wonder and philosophy predates Christianity, I argue that it is only within a Christian framework that the wonder-filled, philosophical life finds its true home.

In chapter 3, I introduce you to an older vision of philosophy as a way of life: an entire way of being in the world that includes the regular practice of spiritual exercises and is therapeutic as it brings greater clarity and health of soul for the sake of living well. In chapter 4, I aim to recover, with the help of Boethius and Lady Philosophy, a Christian philosophical way of life that encompasses not only a view of reality and the good life that is shaped by the Christian story but also one that structures the practices and rhythms of our everyday lives.

In chapter 5, I set out to diagnose two modern existential ailments—our moral and metaphysical vertigo and our loss of sight and attention—that hinder our ability to truly see and orient ourselves to reality as it is. Then, in chapter 6, I show how the Christian philosophical way of life, including various spiritual exercises that make us apt to properly see and attune ourselves to reality, can serve as a strong health-giving remedy for these modern existential ailments.

In chapter 7, I introduce what I call "practicality questions"—questions that orbit around the general suspicion that philosophy is utterly impractical and irrelevant to human life in general and the Christian life in particular (e.g., "What use is philosophy to real life?" "How can philosophy possibly help with discipleship, evangelism, and mission?"). In chapters 7 through 10, I bring to light and critically interact with the following four driving assumptions that often hide behind practicality questions:

- Philosophy is good for nothing (chap. 7).
- If an activity or pursuit is valuable, it's valuable only for the sake of something else (chap. 7).
- An activity is "practical" only if it produces useful, measurable outcomes (chap. 8).
- The Christian life and ministry have nothing to do with the philosophical life and the cultivation of the intellect (chaps. 9–10).

I conclude the book by showing you (and not just telling you) how philosophy can change your life. I briefly explore Augustine's two life-altering interactions with the study of philosophy (one at age eighteen and one at age thirty-one) and examine how philosophical reflection helped tune his discordant mind and heart to be more in harmony with the true and the good. These divinely appointed interactions with the study of philosophy set Augustine on a journey toward the One who is Truth and Goodness itself. And, in all seriousness, there's absolutely no reason why a divinely appointed engagement with philosophy can't change your life too. So let's get to it!

1

An Invitation to Wonder

There are few human experiences quite like that of wonder. Wonder is a distinctively human response to reality, one marked by a deep sense of astonishment, admiration, and awe. We stand in wonder before many things above, below, beyond, and within. We wonder at the mind-boggling immensity of the Grand Canyon below or the starry expanse above, at the momentary flashes of a lightning bug against a dusk sky, at the human genius and achievement that crowns the scientific enterprise, at a courageous act of self-sacrifice, at the timeworn wisdom of a grandparent, at the moral clarity of a friend shaped by great suffering, or at the alluring beauty of a scene from *Les Misérables*.

When we are gripped by wonder, we are startled out of the ordinary and humdrum of human experience. When rightly ordered, wonder can indicate to us that we are in the presence of something truly excellent and worthy of our sustained attention. Wonder is also a window through which we can see reality in its proper light;

what is genuinely good, true, and beautiful—and subsequently worth pursuing—tends to evoke wonder. Wonder brings with it a kind of existential force that propels us beyond the confines of our small, narrow selves and into a much bigger and weightier orbit of reality, into the true depths of things. As Albert Einstein once said, "He who can no longer pause to wonder and stand rapt in awe is as good as dead; his eyes are closed."[1] People who have ceased to wonder have ceased to be gripped by anything bigger than themselves.

Wonder is a distinctively human response precisely because it is a kind of intellectual, moral, and aesthetic response to reality. It is a response to reality that is saturated with intellectual and moral longing and fulfillment: a longing not only to understand but to rest in one's place in the cosmos, a longing not only to discover but to lay hold of deep meaning and purpose in life, to know the ends worth seeking and ultimately to orient one's life to those ends.

The Science of Wonder

But let's slow down a bit and focus in on the following core question: *What exactly is it to wonder or to be in awe?* In recent years, the concept of wonder—both its nature and its personal and social psychological benefits—has been richly explored by contemporary psychologists.[2] According to one leading scientific proposal, experiences of wonder involve two key components: "perceived vastness" and a "need for accommodation." Both components are essential to experiences of wonder. Let's unpack each of these components · in turn.

1. Einstein, from his essay "The World as I See It," quoted in R. Smith, "If Philosophy Begins in Wonder," 93.

2. For a helpful, easy-to-read, popular-level introduction to the psychology of wonder, see Jonah Paquette's book *Awestruck: How Embracing Wonder Can Make You Happier, Healthier, and More Connected* (Boulder, CO: Shambhala, 2020).

In general, when we perceive something as vast, we perceive it as being beyond our current range of experience. As psychologists Dacher Keltner and Jonathan Haidt put it, "Vastness refers to anything that is experienced as being much larger than the self, or the self's ordinary level of experience or frame of reference."[3] We can experience a host of things as vast in this sense. For example, consider an immense physical object (like the Grand Canyon or the Milky Way galaxy), a complex and intricate theoretical concept (the theory of relativity or Gödel's theorem), a person of great prestige or authority or splendor or moral virtue (the late queen of England, Martin Luther King Jr., Mother Teresa), or a beautiful work of art or music (the ceiling of the Sistine Chapel or a performance of Beethoven's Fifth Symphony): we see all of them as being out of the ordinary or even jaw-dropping in memorable ways. Experiencing each of these things tends to elicit wonder precisely because it ushers us into the presence of something much weightier than ourselves that extends beyond our normal experience of the world. I would venture a guess that you've perceived something as vast in this sense at some point in your life. If so, let me encourage you to hold that particular experience of wonder before your mind as we continue.

On its own, though, perceived vastness is not enough to evoke wonder. An experience of wonder also brings with it what Keltner and Haidt call a "need for accommodation." Let me explain. When we experience wonder, our current understanding of the world is shown to be too small or simply inadequate to truly depict what it is that we are experiencing. When this occurs, we are summoned to enlarge the narrow confines of our soul to make room for the new experience and perhaps even to correct the mistaken way that we once viewed the world. This is precisely why we casually describe such experiences as "mind-blowing." When we experience wonder, we

3. Keltner and Haidt, "Approaching Awe," 303.

recognize that the house of our soul is much too small—it has far too few rooms to accommodate what we are encountering in experiences of wonder. What is needed is a soul renovation or remodel, the addition of mental rooms that would allow us to adequately take in what is truly real and worthy of reverence, awe, and careful attention. And when we make the appropriate soul space, the experience of wonder or awe tends to be positive, enlightening, and even soul-satisfying.

We find this dynamic at play in Augustine's *Confessions* when he recognizes the existential smallness of his own self in the presence of the vast immensity of Almighty God: "The house of my soul is too small for you to come to it. May it be enlarged by you."[4] Similarly, when as a kid I first learned of the unfathomable vastness of the universe, I quickly realized that the way I had been thinking about the size of the universe was radically naive and hopelessly mistaken. I learned that the universe was astronomically larger than our own solar system. As my mind expanded to take in a previously unknown truth about the world, I was positively in awe of the sheer immensity of God's physical creation. Indeed, it led me to worship.

We Are Wonder-Hungry

Human beings have a unique appetite for wonder; we are wonder-hungry, we might say. In fact, some people pay millions of dollars to chase experiences of wonder and awe. Consider the recent advent of space tourism, led by companies such as Blue Dot, SpaceX, and Virgin Galactic. People can now pay multimillions of dollars to experience minutes of weightlessness and a glimpse of the earth from a vantage point at the edge of space. Even NASA, which once opposed the idea of space tourism, has recently announced that for a whopping $55 million per ticket, civilians may visit the International Space Station.

4. Augustine, *Confessions* 1.6, p. 6.

But what exactly is the lure of space tourism? The emotion astronauts experience upon seeing the earth from space might give us a clue. Researchers call this experience the "overview effect." Listen to NASA astronaut Samuel Durrance explain the overview effect: "You've seen pictures and you've heard people talk about it. But nothing can prepare you for what it actually looks like. The Earth is dramatically beautiful when you see it from orbit, more beautiful than any picture you've ever seen. It's an emotional experience because you're removed from the Earth but at the same time you feel this incredible connection to the Earth like nothing I'd ever felt before."[5] We find both features of wonder on display in the overview effect: perceived vastness and need for accommodation. (Can you spot them both in the Durrance quotation?)

Of course, the overview effect represents an extremely rare experience of wonder and awe that few of us will have the opportunity to call our own. But we all know, deep down, that you don't have to be a multimillionaire to experience wonder. You don't have to be part of a certain socioeconomic class to experience the world in jaw-dropping and soul-satisfying ways. In fact, your feet don't even have to leave the surface of the earth. And this is very good news for those of us who are not multimillionaires!

The reality is that creation above and below is truly *wonder*ful in itself precisely *because* it is the creative product and reflection of the triune God, a being who is infinitely vast, more beautiful than the totality of creation itself. Because of what creation *is*—the workmanship and reflection of the triune God—there will always be a rich surplus of earthly goods to contemplate and lovingly attend to as we await the *wonder*ful and soul-satisfying vision of creation's artist in the life to come.

In the meantime, whether we lovingly ponder the face of a newborn child, the aged wisdom of a grandparent forged through a life

---

5. This quotation from Durrance is located in Yaden et al., "Overview Effect," 2.

of trial and suffering, or the grandeur of the Grand Tetons, we can catch momentary and wonderful glimpses of the goodness, wisdom, and grandeur of the triune God. Creation's intrinsic capacity to evoke wonder is available to all of us, irrespective of annual salary and social status. All that is needed is the uniquely human ability to *see* reality in its proper light—as suffused with truth, goodness, and beauty in every nook and cranny. And, as we will see in the chapters to come, this is precisely what the Christian philosophical way of life is all about: cultivating the capacity to see reality in all its fullness and orienting one's life to it accordingly.

Wonder Is Good for You: The Psychological Benefits of Wonder

For the Christian, experiences of wonder are available to all those who have cultivated the ability to see reality for what it is and in its proper light. And the reason this is good news may surprise you: *wonder is actually good for you.* What exactly do I mean? Psychologists have been able to identify several positive individual and social effects of wonder, effects that increase one's overall psychological well-being and social connectedness. Let me introduce you to a few of wonder's most important psychological benefits.

The most studied psychological benefit of wonder is what researchers call "the small-self effect." According to a leading scientific proposal on the psychological benefits of wonder, regular experiences of wonder tend to make us feel small, both in a physical sense (as when we stand before the Pacific Ocean or the Grand Canyon) and in the sense of being less concerned with our own selves and more concerned with the world around us, including the interests of others.[6] In other words, wonder tends to decrease our sense of

6. Perlin and Li, "Why Does Awe Have Prosocial Effects?"

self-importance and make us more open and responsive to the world around us.

One well-known study of wonder's small-self effect had 1,178 tourists (from seventy-six different countries of origin) report their feelings of awe and wonder along with their perceived sense of self. To help measure feelings of wonder and sense of self, researchers asked tourists to draw a picture of themselves and to report their perceived "self-size" by means of a series of circles increasing in size.[7] The study drew on tourists who visited either Yosemite National Park or Fisherman's Wharf in San Francisco (if you've never been to either place, pause and take a moment to do a web search for a sense of reference). Interestingly, after visiting Yosemite National Park, one of the most awe-inspiring places on the planet, tourists from a wide range of cultural backgrounds reported experiencing significantly more awe and chose smaller circles to represent their sense of self than did the tourists who visited Fisherman's Wharf. In fact, the self-portraits of the tourists who visited Yosemite were nearly 33 percent smaller than those of the tourists who visited Fisherman's Wharf. What's even more interesting is that researchers found that this small-self effect in the presence of something wonderful and awe-inspiring was more prevalent among tourists from more individualistic cultures, such as the United States and Europe, than it was for tourists from more collectivist cultures, such as those of East Asia.

A second benefit of wonder, closely related to the small-self effect and to viewing wonder as a "self-transcendent" emotion,[8] is that the regular experience of wonder can help cultivate humility. Regular experiences of wonder can guard against the temptation to think that we are masters and possessors of nature and that our primary posture toward God's creation is one of control and manipulation

7. Bai et al., "Awe, the Diminished Self, and Collective Engagement."
8. Yaden et al., "Overview Effect," 5.

rather than appreciation and acceptance. Wonder can help put us more in touch with our "existential limits," we might say.[9] Many experiences of wonder put us in contact with realities that are truly awe-inspiring and worthy of reverence and respect. Such experiences also remind us that our own existence is fragile and radically dependent on factors that are largely outside our control. Summarizing one particular psychological study along these lines, neuroscientist and popular science writer Summer Allen notes, "This study found that people who are more dispositionally prone to experiencing awe were rated as more humble by their friends; people who reported feeling more awe over the course of two weeks also reported feeling more humble; and experimentally inducing awe in participants led them to 'present a more balanced view of their strengths and weaknesses to others and acknowledge, to a greater degree, the contribution of outside forces in their own personal accomplishments.'"[10] As a self-transcendent emotion, wonder can remind us of our proper place in the cosmos, both with respect to God and with respect to others, as well as of the natural, God-given limits within which we fully thrive as humans.

This diminished sense of self and increased openness to the world can lead to a third benefit of wonder: a greater sense of connectedness with our surroundings and with others, including our friends and larger social communities. This effect was clear in the case of the "overview effect"—that is, the experience of wonder in seeing the earth from the vantage point of space. Recall the words of astronaut Samuel Durrance concerning the overview effect: "You feel this incredible connection to the Earth like nothing I'd ever felt before."[11]

9. See McPherson, *Virtues of Limits*, chap. 1. I borrow the phrase "existential limits" from McPherson.
10. S. Allen, "Science of Awe," 28. The internal quotation is from Stellar et al., "Awe and Humility."
11. See Yaden et al., "Overview Effect," 2.

The idea that experiences of wonder tend to foster a greater sense of connectedness to others finds support in a study similar to the one described above regarding the small-self effect. In a study of 242 participants, researchers measured the effect of wonder on people's sense of connectedness to a greater whole or to a particular community. Participants were presented with a series of six pairs of circles: one circle in each pair was labeled "self" and the other "community." On one end of the series the two circles do not overlap at all, and at the other end the two circles almost entirely overlap.[12] Participants were randomly assigned to describe a recent experience of wonder ("in the presence of something or someone that is so great in terms of size or intensity that their current understanding of the world, their surroundings, or themselves is challenged in some way"), a recent experience of shame ("a painful feeling of humiliation or distress caused by the consciousness of wrong or foolish behavior"), or a neutral experience ("the last time you did laundry"). People were then asked to choose the pair of circles that best captured their sense of self in relation to their wider community. And yes, you guessed it: the participants who reflected on a recent experience of wonder chose circles that overlapped more than those who reflected on a shameful or neutral experience.

The researchers who conducted the study note the close connection between the small-self effect and a greater sense of connectedness to others: "Experiences of awe diminish the sense of the self, enabling more collective engagement." In fact, this is precisely why some psychologists refer to wonder or awe as a "self-transcendent emotion" and to experiences of wonder as "self-transcendent experiences," since wonder tends to draw us out of ourselves and more firmly connect us to the world around us.[13] In short, psychological

---

12. Mashek, Cannaday, and Tangney, "Inclusion of Community in Self Scale."
13. Yaden et al., "Overview Effect."

science suggests that the regular experience of wonder can open us up to reality by making us less self-oriented and more others-oriented.

A fourth and final benefit of wonder, one that will serve as a helpful transition to our discussion of the essential role of wonder in the philosophical life, is that wonder fosters a greater desire for intellectual exploration and understanding. Recall that experiences of wonder involve the need for a renovation or enlargement of the soul to make room for the object of wonder ("need for accommodation"). In experiences of wonder, we encounter something, someone, or some place that boggles the mind and defies our current intellectual grasp of reality. And, more often than not, the resulting intellectual tension in the wake of such experiences of wonder leads to a greater desire to make sense of our experience of the world. As one researcher put it, "The feeling of uncertainty created by this gap between knowledge and experience triggers a need for accommodation (or knowledge restructuring) that promotes explanation and exploration, two crucial antecedents of learning."[14] While psychologists have pointed to the benefits of wonder in helping facilitate scientific reasoning and learning in particular, these benefits can be applied more broadly to intellectual exploration in general, including philosophical, scientific, and theological exploration alike. Psychological science suggests that when we regularly experience wonder, we are more prone to seek explanations and to make proper sense of the world around us.

We've been talking a lot about the specific personal and social psychological benefits of wonder. But what sorts of situations or experiences tend to evoke wonder? Psychologists have identified several types of stimuli that are most likely to evoke wonder, what psychologists call "awe elicitors." The most significant and frequent awe elicitors are those that tend to be "information rich"—that is,

14. Valdesolo, Shtulman, and Baron, "Science Is Awe-Some," quoted in S. Allen, "Science of Awe," 34.

those that are perceptually or theoretically complex enough to create the needed tension within our current understanding of the world. This falls in line with one of the two essential ingredients of wonder described above: the need for accommodation. Along these lines, psychologists have pointed to the natural world, music, art, and spiritual and religious experiences as stimuli that tend to evoke wonder more than other stimuli, precisely because of their inherent vastness and complexity. And, as we will see in the next chapter, philosophical exploration has traditionally been viewed as an awe elicitor.

2

Wonder as the Lifeblood of Philosophy

We Philosophize Because We Are Human

Our best psychological science tells us that we are wonder-hungry and that the regular experience of wonder is actually good for us, both individually and socially. One primary way in which our wonder hunger has manifested itself throughout history has been in our collective desire as a species to make ultimate sense of things, to philosophize. In this way, we might even think that a desire to philosophize is as natural to us as our desire to eat, drink, and live in community. The desires to eat, drink, and live in community are all expressions and fulfillments of our natural human inclinations as *rational* and *social* animals. As rational animals, material creatures that have been gifted with an immaterial, rational soul, we are created with both a physical hunger to satisfy our material needs and a deep metaphysical hunger to satisfy our spiritual and intellectual needs, to make ultimate sense of things and to feed upon truth. Humans, by nature, crave truth and understanding. This is precisely what Aristotle meant when he famously said at the outset of his *Metaphysics*, "All men by nature desire to know."[1] The philosophical quest is a uniquely *human* quest. Humans are set apart from all other living creatures by our built-in appetite for truth, for meaning, and for properly understanding reality. We are "meaning-seeking animals" in that we strive, by nature, to make sense of things, ultimately for the purpose of living well.[2] And we strive to make sense not just of some part of reality in isolation from everything else, such as geography or economics. Rather, we naturally seek to make sense of *the totality of things and how everything fits together, for the purpose of living well.*

According to a time-tested understanding of philosophy, this is precisely what the philosophical quest is all about. A desire to know and fit oneself into reality as a whole—to be at home in the world at large—is the very substance of the philosophical life. As one philosopher put it, "Philosophy asks the simple question: what is it all about?"[3] If you've ever stopped to ponder the meaning of it all, or even the meaning of your own life and how it fits into the larger story of reality, you've taken a few small steps along the philosophical path.

Whether we realize it or not, we all carry around what philosopher Mary Midgley calls "world-pictures." World-pictures are "perspectives, imaginative visions of how the whole world is."[4] These imaginative visions are like existential maps or "cosmic outlooks"[5] that orient us to reality at large, and they always include a "you are

1. *Metaphysics* 1.1 (980a), in Aristotle, *New Aristotle Reader*, 255.
2. I borrow the phrase "meaning-seeking animals" from McPherson, *Virtue and Meaning*. McPherson borrows it from Sacks, *Great Partnership*, chap. 1.
3. Whitehead, "Remarks," 178.
4. Midgley, *What Is Philosophy For?*, 73, quoted in McPherson, *Virtue and Meaning*, 168.
5. McPherson, *Virtue and Meaning*, chap. 4.

here" point of reference that indicates where we think we are in light of our entire map of reality. Odds are that few of us have stopped to carefully consider the adequacy of our current world-pictures or existential maps (including whether where we *think* we are is where we *actually* are). Rather, most of us passively absorb these world-pictures or existential maps like a sponge, mostly from our cultural surroundings, including key culture-shaping institutions such as the family, the church, the education system, the government, and the entertainment industry.

The unfortunate truth is that few of us will slow down long enough to carefully evaluate the merits of our world-pictures or existential maps, whether they are true to reality or not; only a small minority of us will take more than a few steps along the path of the examined, philosophical life. Indeed, for most of us, strolling along the path of the examined life is simply too demanding on our attention, our time, our loves, our very lives. In an age in which the "desires of the eyes" reign supreme (1 John 2:16), carefully cultivating the ability to see reality *as it truly is* (rather than *how I desire it to be*) loses much of its motivation and allure. When getting retweeted, getting reelected, or getting a raise is more important to us than getting reality right and fitting ourselves into it, we know we've lost our way.

But it is vital that we learn to linger along the philosophical path once again by subjecting our cherished existential maps to intellectual scrutiny. And why, exactly, is it so important to evaluate the merits of our current existential maps? Because at the end of the day, the purpose of a map—whether a map of New York City or Disneyland or an existential map of reality and our place in it—is for accurate and successful navigation. World-pictures are "the necessary background of all our living."[6]

---

6. Midgley, *What Is Philosophy For?*, 73.

So the purpose of evaluating the merits of our existential maps is so that we can accurately and successfully navigate life itself. In the end, we want an existential map to help us navigate the world in such a way that we leave the harbor of moral and intellectual immaturity (Eph. 4:11–16), remain seaworthy and majestic amid life's disorienting swells, avoid running aground on the jagged rocks of life, and successfully reach our final destination. If a mistaken or unreliable nautical map can lead to disorienting and even life-destroying results (being adrift at sea with no sense of where the shore is or what dangers need to be avoided), *how much more* will a mistaken or unreliable existential map lead to devastating existential disorientation? As the apostle Paul put it regarding two men he knew (Hymenaeus and Alexander), living in accordance with the wrong existential map "made shipwreck of their faith" (1 Tim. 1:19).

We might even say that to suppress or ignore the natural desire to make sense of life as a whole—to live the examined human life, to philosophize—is in deep tension with our God-given nature as meaning-seeking animals. While Socrates's famous statement that "the unexamined life is not worth living" is perhaps overly strong, it does point to the important truth that philosophy "is a profoundly human endeavor as it is connected to our being the meaning-seeking animal, and when properly pursued it is also a humanizing endeavor, that is, it realizes an integrally important feature of our humanity."[7]

Since we are meaning-seeking animals by nature, our natural appetite to "make sense of it all" is not the sort of hunger we can choose to take up and put down as we see fit—no more than we can dispense with our natural appetite for food when we wish to do so. While we don't choose our natural appetite for food, we can certainly choose not to eat, and this would be devasting to our human existence as

---

7. McPherson, *Virtue and Meaning*, 168. I share McPherson's worry that Socrates's statement is a bit too strong as stated.

biological creatures. In the same way, while we don't choose our natural appetite to make sense of it all—to philosophize—we can certainly choose not to feed upon truth and understanding, which would be equally devasting to our human existence as *intellectual* creatures. In this way, "to engage in philosophy means to reflect on the totality of things we encounter, in view of their ultimate reasons; and philosophy, thus understood, is a meaningful, even necessary endeavor, with which man, the spiritual being, cannot dispense."[8] To strive to make sense of it all and to orient one's life accordingly—to philosophize—is both unique and indispensable to human existence.

The idea of clearly seeing and fitting oneself into reality at large is also an important aspect of a biblical conception of *wisdom*. Biblically, wisdom is rightly seeing and rightly living along the grain of reality; it is being skilled at the art of living. Just as a piece of wood has a natural grain to it, created reality likewise has a natural grain to it. The wise person seeks to know and to live *along* the grain of reality, and the foolish person seeks to ignore and to live *against* the grain of reality. And the stakes are high indeed. When we fail to clearly discern the natural grain of reality (whether because of ignorance or willful suppression), we perish (Hosea 4:6). In fact, according to Scripture, the person who fails to discern the grain of reality and to walk in the way of wisdom loves death and "injures himself" (Prov. 8:36).

One of the most helpful characterizations of biblical wisdom that I've come across is from theologian J. I. Packer: "Wisdom is the power to see, and the inclination to choose, the best and highest goal, together with the surest means of attaining it."[9] I suggest that you pause and read Packer's definition again—it is deeply insightful. Wisdom is not merely cerebral or intellectual; being wise is not the same thing as getting a PhD, successfully gathering information, solving mental

---

8. Pieper, *In Defense of Philosophy*, 12.
9. Packer, *Knowing God*, quoted in Deweese, *Doing Philosophy as a Christian*, 51.

puzzles, receiving a high score on an IQ test, or even seeing how a list of facts hangs together. Rather, wisdom is an orientation of the whole person: the mind, the will, and the actions. Biblically speaking, the wise person's *head*, *heart*, and *hands* are rightly oriented to what is genuinely true, good, and beautiful.

But of course, for the Christian philosopher, wisdom—and with it the notion of philosophy as the love and active pursuit of wisdom—ultimately centers on the eternal Word of God, Jesus Christ, "the power of God and the wisdom of God" (1 Cor. 1:24). In fact, the apostle Paul notes that the full riches and embodiment of wisdom are rooted in Christ, "in whom are hidden all the treasures of wisdom and knowledge" (Col. 2:3). Jesus, as the eternal "wisdom of God," is the agent and archetype of all creation; all creation finds its creative origin and deepest meaning in the person of Jesus Christ. As a newly built home finds its ultimate origin and meaning in the mental image of a human architect, so too creation finds its ultimate origin and meaning in the eternal Word, "the image of the invisible God" by whom "all things were created, in heaven and on earth, visible and invisible, whether thrones or dominions or rulers or authorities—all things were created through him and for him. And he is before all things, and in him all things hold together" (Col. 1:15–17).

Since every aspect of created reality has been fashioned *by* and *for* Christ as the very wisdom of God, to know and live in accordance with creation's natural grain is to know and live in accordance with his good purposes for creation. As lovers of Christ, who himself is the storehouse of all the treasures of wisdom and knowledge, Christian philosophers should lovingly attend to his wise workmanship on display in creation, including the moral contours and natural grain of creation itself.

Consider how Christian theologian Cornelius Plantinga Jr. unpacks the connection between knowing and loving the natural grain of creation and knowing and loving God:

In the literature of Scripture, wisdom is, broadly speaking, the knowledge of God's world and the knack of fitting oneself into it. The wise person knows creation. She knows its boundaries and limits, understands its laws and rhythms, discerns its times and seasons, respects its great dynamics. She understands that creation possesses its own integrity and significance quite apart from her claim on it and quite apart from any possibility that creation will make her happy. The wise person gives in to creation and to God—and she does the first because she does the second.[10]

Thus, Christian philosophers in particular should strive to know, to respect, and to "give in" to the natural grain of created reality—its boundaries and limits (including the boundaries and limits of human nature) and its laws and rhythms (including the laws and rhythms of the moral life, what is truly morally fulfilling and truly morally destructive for humans). And they do this precisely *because* they strive to know, respect, and "give in" to the triune God. This is precisely why "the fear of the LORD is the beginning of wisdom" (Prov. 9:10). Without being rightly oriented to God in mind and heart, it is impossible for the philosopher to be rightly oriented to the natural grain of reality at large, as genuine wisdom requires.

Wonder as the Lifeblood of Philosophy

To philosophize as a Christian, then, is to strive both to attune oneself to what *is* and *ought to be* in Christ and to orient one's life accordingly. We can now begin to see the close connection between wonder and the Christian philosophical life, a life-posture that is marked by a habitual openness and orientation to what is genuinely true, good, and beautiful in the light of Christ.

10. Plantinga, *Not the Way It's Supposed to Be*, 115.

Indeed, we might even say that "the inner form of philosophizing is virtually identical with the inner form of wonder."[11] What exactly does this mean? It means that the experience of wonder and the activity of philosophizing as a Christian have very similar features. As is the case with wonder, both *perceived vastness* and *a need for accommodation* are essential ingredients of the philosophical life.

Let's start with perceived vastness (whether physical or conceptual). Here we must tread carefully, since the vastness perceived in philosophizing need not involve something that is always *over and against* what we normally consider mundane and ordinary to human life and experience. Rather, perceiving something as vast by means of Christian philosophical reflection may involve perceiving the ordinary and mundane in its true light, in all its existential richness and complexity, illuminated by the radiance and light of God in Christ.

To philosophize as a Christian, then, is to see the inner depth, the meaning, and the ultimate purpose of created things, including (perhaps especially) the ordinary and mundane, ultimately in light of their true meaning in Christ. When the Christian leans further into the philosophical posture in this sense, the ordinary and mundane "lose their density and solidity and their apparent finality—they can no longer be taken for granted. Things then assume a strange, new, and deeper aspect." The act of philosophizing as a Christian is never just "business as usual," we might say. Far from being a posture of retreat from the "real world," as is commonly thought, Christian philosophical reflection strives to see and interact with reality at large, including the ordinary and mundane, *as it truly is*. When a Christian sets out to philosophize, they "withdraw not from the things of everyday life, but from the currently accepted meaning attached to them, or to question the value placed upon them."[12]

11. Pieper, *Philosophical Act*, 116.
12. Pieper, *Philosophical Act*, 110.

A second similarity between the experience of wonder and the act of philosophizing involves the need for accommodation. As with wonder, philosophical reflection, at its best, invites a renovation of our existing mental space and how we conceive of the world, including our understanding of the nature of reality and the purpose for which it exists. As we've already seen, when we wonder we encounter something—a person, place, or idea—that rattles and challenges the mind in a way that presses against our current intellectual grasp of the world. We are invited to begin to make the necessary space in our souls to house a reality that turns out to be much bigger and more complex than we initially realized. As we've already seen, experiences of wonder foster a greater desire to understand and make sense of the world of our experience. Wonder invites a greater fit between reality *as it actually is* and reality *as I believe it to be*. It can shift us out of intellectual neutral and into a gear that drives us forward in the examined life, the distinctively human life. In light of the close similarities between wonder and the act of philosophizing, we might summarize the Christian philosophical life as a life that is devoted to cultivating a deep sense of the wonder of it all, ultimately in light of the true meaning and purpose of all created things in Christ.

Up to this point we have been exploring the close structural similarities between wonder and philosophy in that they both involve perceived vastness and a need for accommodation. But here I want to point out the rich historical precedent for viewing wonder as *the* lifeblood of the philosophical life. The idea that there is a close connection between wonder and philosophy is as old as philosophical reflection itself. While the intimate connection between wonder and philosophy finds its origin in the pre-Christian thought of Plato and Aristotle and thus is not exclusively Christian, I will aim to show that the connection finds its natural home in the Christian theological tradition. Indeed, I want to suggest something stronger: only within a Christian conception of reality is the wonder-filled philosophical life possible.

So let's take a brief look at some representative examples of the connection between wonder and philosophy in the history of Western philosophy. Plato (ca. 428–348 BC), who is rightly called the father of Western philosophy, strongly underscores the relationship between philosophy and wonder. In Plato's dialogue *Theaetetus*, Socrates puts his finger on wonder as the fundamental motivation and affective drive underlying the love and pursuit of wisdom: "For this is an experience which is characteristic of a philosopher, this wondering: this is where philosophy begins and nowhere else."[13] The distinctive mark of a philosopher, for Socrates, is the experience of wonder. Likewise, Aristotle, Plato's best student (384–322 BC), echoes his teacher on this in his *Metaphysics* when he says, "For it is owing to their wonder that men both now begin and at first began to philosophize."[14] Representing the classical Christian tradition is the great theologian and philosopher Thomas Aquinas (AD 1225–1274), who, following in footsteps of this age-old tradition, said that "those who first philosophized and who now philosophize did so from wonder."[15] For these pagan and Christian philosophical heavyweights, "to perceive all that is unusual and exceptional, all that is wonderful, in the midst of the ordinary things of everyday life, is the beginning of philosophy."[16]

But philosophy not only begins in wonder, it is also sustained by and brought to completion in wonder. As we will see in more detail in the next chapter, wonder for the philosopher is more like an enduring, stable *posture*—a way of life—than a passing, momentary *state*. The influential German philosopher Martin Heidegger (1889–1976), commenting on the above remarks from Plato and Aristotle about the

---

13. *Theaetetus*, in *Plato: Complete Works*, 173.
14. *Metaphysics* 1.2 (982b), in Aristotle, *New Aristotle Reader*, 258.
15. Thomas Aquinas, *Commentary on the Metaphysics of Aristotle* 1.3.
16. Pieper, *Philosophical Act*, 113.

historically prominent relationship between philosophy and wonder, makes this important point well:

> Astonishment . . . is the *arche* [underlying principle] of philosophy. . . . Astonishment thus does not simply stand at the beginning of philosophy, as, for example, the washing of his hands precedes the surgeon's operation. Astonishment carries and pervades philosophy. . . . It would be very superficial and, above all, un-Greek, if we would believe that Plato and Aristotle are only determining here that astonishment is the cause of philosophizing. If they were of this opinion, that would mean that at some time or other men were astonished especially about being and that it is and what it is. Impelled by this astonishment, they began to philosophize. As soon as philosophy was in progress, astonishment became superfluous as a propelling force so that it disappeared. It could disappear since it was only an impetus. However, astonishment is *arche*—it pervades every step of philosophy.[17]

For Heidegger, just as blood permeates every vein of the human body, astonishment (wonder) is the very lifeblood of philosophy from beginning to end.

For a variety of reasons (apathy, neglect, diversions), our capacity to experience wonder tends to gradually diminish with time and age. Yet reality itself never ceases to retain its God-given capacity to awe, astonish, and mystify those who are willing and able to see. For Heidegger, the astonishment and wonder that first awakens us out of the slumber of the unexamined life is the very same astonishment and wonder that propels us ever forward in the examined life. As the philosopher Alfred N. Whitehead (1861–1947) put it, "at the end, when philosophic thought has done its best, the wonder remains."[18] Wonder, from beginning to end.

17. Heidegger, "What Is Philosophy," quoted in R. Smith, "If Philosophy Begins in Wonder," 93.
18. Whitehead, *Modes of Thought*, as quoted in R. Smith, "If Philosophy Begins in Wonder," 92.

Does this conception of philosophy as a wonder-driven enterprise fit with the conception you currently hold in your mind? If so, great; if not, then I hope you'll at least be open to considering a different view, one that I'll be exploring throughout this book. In general, then, and contrary to a common misperception of philosophy in the public imagination, philosophical reflection ought not first and foremost to be motivated by idle speculation or a desire to intellectually outwit others, or by a lucrative academic post at an Ivy League institution, or by a desire to gain cultural influence by way of intellectual superiority. Believe it or not, the philosophical life ought not to be motivated even by the chance to wear tweed blazers and to work in messy university offices surrounded by stacks of books and papers (though I'm a big fan of tweed and books myself).

This, of course, is not to say that philosophical reflection is never pursued or taught in such a way that positively diminishes wonder. The fact is that while the philosophical enterprise can be and increasingly is lured away by these misdirected motivations and aims, historically it was understood to properly begin with a deep sense of the wonder of it all.

Christianity and the Wonder-Filled, Philosophical Life

So we've seen that wonder and philosophy are joined at the hip and have traditionally been so joined from antiquity. Wonder and philosophy are inseparable activities, both of which are unique and indispensable to a rich and meaningful human existence. While the wonder-philosophy connection is not distinctively Christian in origin, I now want to unpack why I think the connection finds its true and natural home within Christianity in particular. There are three Christian theological insights that I think make the wonder-filled, philosophical life possible in the first place: theological anthropology, the nature of creation itself, and the close fit between human cognitive abilities and our appetite to make sense of and understand the world. Let's unpack each of these in turn.

We've already seen that psychological science suggests that wonder is good for us, both individually and collectively. But, for the Christian, is this really all that surprising? I think not, precisely because I believe there's a deeper theological reason for thinking that we were made to wonder, which leads to the first insight from anthropology that makes the wonder-filled, philosophical life possible: *we were made for God*. And God, of course, is vast beyond measure, not *quantitatively* (size-wise, we might say) but *qualitatively* in the sense that the infinite fullness of God's triune life is beyond our ordinary level of experience or frame of reference. While we may be tempted to think that we've fully comprehended the fullness and immensity of God's life—that we've got God hemmed in or that we've become masters of divinity—we most certainly have not; nor is this even possible, given who God is.

You were made, then, as a key is made for a lock, to forever know and love and enjoy a Being who is immeasurably vast beyond complete human comprehension. And this deep truth about God is precisely why there will always be aspects of our ongoing knowledge and experience of God (both in this life and in the life to come) that require constant mental accommodation on our behalf, new things we learn and experience in our continued life with God that we will need to make room for within the narrow halls of our little minds. By God's own design, we will be eternally awestruck by the vastness, splendor, and beauty of the triune God and the wonderful works of his hands. In the end, our wonder hunger is not the product of purely unguided evolutionary processes. By design, we were made to wonder.

Precisely because we were made for God, a being that is infinitely, qualitatively vast and beyond full human comprehension, we were made to wonder. And because of the close connection between wonder and philosophy—wonder is the beginning, middle, and end of the philosophical life—we might even say that we were made to live the philosophical life, to seek to make meaningful and intelligible sense of it all (ultimately in light of Christ), and to orient our lives accordingly.

And this leads to the second Christian theological insight that makes the wonder-filled, philosophical life possible: creation itself is the proper object of wonder precisely *because* every facet of it communicates and reflects the marvelous truth, goodness, and beauty of its triune Creator. A robust, even sacramental, doctrine of creation provides a fitting, theological basis for an earthly posture of philosophical wonder. Since all creaturely reality originates in, is sustained by, and finds it proper end in the triune God (Col. 1:16–17; Rom. 11:36), deep attention to created reality is ultimately a God-directed activity.

The created order's capacity to reflect and point toward the triune God in some way or other has been an important aspect of the doctrine of creation throughout the Christian tradition, past and present. While there are many representatives of a sacramental or communicative understanding of creation throughout patristic, medieval, Reformed, and contemporary Christian thought, let me mention just one.

The idea that creation is communicative of the divine can be found in the work of the Protestant reformer John Calvin (1509–1564), who himself was steeped in the thought of the early church fathers.[19] Calvin noted that God "daily discloses himself in the whole workmanship of the universe" and that creation is a "sort of mirror in which we can contemplate God, who is otherwise invisible." For Calvin, God has "engraved unmistakable marks of his glory" on each and every aspect of his creative work.[20]

---

19. See Lane, *John Calvin*.
20. Calvin, *Institutes of the Christian Religion*, 52, 53.

As one might expect, Calvin was of the mind that an in-depth study of "astronomy, medicine, and the natural sciences" helps foster a deeper knowledge of these etchings of divine glory in creation. More striking is the fact that Calvin was adamant that those "who have either quaffed or even tasted the liberal arts penetrate with their aid *far more deeply* into the secrets of the divine wisdom."[21]

Calvin's point here can be easily missed, so let's slow down to make sure that we don't miss it. For Calvin, the study of the liberal arts enables one to see *clearer* and *further into* the treasures of divine wisdom—*even more so than the study of the natural sciences*. Indeed, cultivating a greater capacity to see the glory of God on display in creation *by way of the liberal arts* is ultimately for the purpose of savoring God, "to lead [the inquirer] to break forth in admiration of the Artificer."[22] As with all Christian intellectual inquiry, the philosophical study of the good, the true, and the beautiful is ordered first to wonder and, ultimately, to the admiration of God.

Before you read further, let me encourage you to pause to consider this remarkable claim by Calvin, particularly in light of the current crisis of the liberal arts in a context in which higher education is dominated by STEM disciplines (science, technology, engineering, and mathematics). I know of no better defense of the study of the liberal arts (including philosophy) in the midst of our distorted, consumer-driven approach to higher education than this: the liberal arts can give us eyes to see more clearly the divine beauty, goodness, and wisdom on display in creation, for the sake of a greater delight in and admiration of God.

As with all Christian intellectual endeavors, Christian philosophical reflection should be a single movement of awe and astonishment that finds its origin in created things and its final completion in the

21. Calvin, *Institutes of the Christian Religion*, 53 (emphasis added).
22. Calvin, *Institutes of the Christian Religion*, 53.

uncreated Cause from whom, through whom, and to whom are all things. As the British author and poet Samuel Taylor Coleridge (1772–1834) so eloquently put it, "In wonder all philosophy began, in wonder it ends, and admiration fills up the interspace; but the first wonder is the offspring of ignorance, the last is the parent of adoration."[23]

The third and final Christian theological insight that makes the wonder-filled philosophical life possible involves a truth about us together with a truth about the rest of creation: we were made with the unique ability to intellectually grasp reality and thus experience wonder. Not only is creation itself—from the ordinary to the extraordinary—suffused with the awe-inspiring radiance of the triune God, but we were created with the specific intellectual equipment to reliably discern this radiance. There is, you might say, a natural fit between our intellectual capacity to wonder and the remarkable fact that reality itself is, in all its dimensions, truly wonder*ful*. As a key is made specifically for a lock, we were specifically made to apprehend the marvelous contours of reality. We were made to discern and fit ourselves into the creational patterns and rhythms that exist for God's glory and our moral good.

The fact that humans are uniquely endowed with the right cognitive equipment for reliable and successful intellectual exploration— whether by way of the natural sciences or by way of philosophical reflection—is certainly no cosmic accident. The Christian story provides a natural place for this truth about the tight fit of our intellectual abilities to experience wonder with the fact that creation itself is truly *wonder*ful and marvelous. You were specifically made to marvel, to see and savor the truth, goodness, and beauty of God as well as the marvelous works of his hands.

---

23. Coleridge, *Aids to Reflection*, as quoted in R. Smith, "If Philosophy Begins in Wonder," 94.

Let me encourage you to pause and think about this remarkable truth for a moment: God has set the stage for us to experience a life of soul-satisfying wonder. He has done this by creating us with the unique capacity to know and be enthralled by his vastness (theological anthropology), both now and forever, by giving us a front-row seat in the theater of his radiant glory (creation) and by endowing us with the specific intellectual equipment to lovingly behold it all in contemplation (the fit between us and creation). So I ask, What are we waiting for?

3

Philosophy as a Way of Life

Philosophy's Public Relations Problem

I've tried to put before you a vision of philosophy that is uniquely and inescapably human and that has wonder as its very lifeblood from beginning to end. Yet philosophy in general tends to have a public relations problem today, as noted in the introduction. I know this from personal experience, including countless conversations with family, friends, and strangers about my own vocation as a Christian philosopher. Many required college philosophy courses are downright boring and completely out of touch with questions of real, human importance. Believe it or not, I dropped my first college philosophy course for just this reason. And I can't tell you how many times I've heard others convey the exact same experience as mine.

At best, many people—both Christian and non-Christian, academic and nonacademic—are woefully underinformed about what philosophy is, let alone what it is for. At worst, many people—across diverse generational, economic, political, and religious spectrums— conceive of philosophers as rather cartoonish figures, fumbling about in their libraries in their wrinkled sport coats, looking as if they are not sure which way is up and which way is down. Some of these conceptions are well deserved, while others are not. (I know countless academic philosophers who are more in tune with the world than most people are.)

And when the reclusive and rather socially awkward specimens we call philosophers do emerge from their cave of books to give a lecture on Plato's forms or Kant's categorical imperative, it becomes increasingly clear to many that these men and women are quickly becoming intellectual relics of a bygone age. Philosophers are masters of an ancient craft that has been far surpassed by more "relevant" disciplines—STEM disciplines (science, technology, engineering, and math)—that lead to "real" discoveries about the world, discoveries that better the human condition and help us live well. And the reality is that this ignorance (at best) and cartoonish conception (at worst) of philosophy and philosophers is shared by far too many Christians. Herein lies philosophy's contemporary public relations problem.

Recovering Philosophy as a Way of Life

But what if there's a different way to think about philosophy as a Christian—a more robust, ancient way? Indeed there is, and in this chapter I'd like to try to reorient the way you think about philosophy, whether you're a philosophical novice or a philosophical veteran. So let's get to it!

I suspect that most of us are in some sense familiar with the important difference between an activity one engages in every now and then and an activity that is woven into the fabric of one's life, a *way of life*. I'm often confronted with this difference when someone visits my home and sees a guitar in my study, which inevitably leads them to infer, not unreasonably, that I am a musician. But I am no such thing. When they ask me whether I'm a musician, I say no every time, without fail. Don't get me wrong: I enjoy playing the guitar every now and then. I even wrote a song or two for my wife some years back. But playing music is not an activity that is woven into the fabric of my life; *music is not a way of life for me.* I say this precisely because I know many who actually are musicians. For musicians, writing, performing, practicing, and teaching music are some of the steady rhythms of their lives; they live a musical kind of life, we might say.

The same could be said about being a runner, being a reader, or being a surfer. Unless running, reading, and surfing are activities that are intricately woven into the fabric and substance of your life, you may not rightly claim such titles as your own. While you might enjoy running every now and then, this does not warrant calling yourself a runner. While you might enjoy reading a book on the beach or catching some waves on your yearly beach vacation, these one-off activities do not warrant calling yourself a reader or a surfer.

What's the relevant difference here? Running, reading, and surfing considered as *ways of life* are not defined by moments sprinkled throughout one's life; rather, they are defined by an enduring and pervasive *way of being in the world.* This way of being is marked not only by the activities in question but also by disciplined practices, priorities, and sacrifices—and by careful attention to what is needed to successfully carry out the relevant activities (e.g., running *well*, reading *well*, and surfing *well*). For example, in addition to regularly running, those who pursue the running kind of life organize a great deal of their lives around the craft of running, ultimately for the purpose of running well. Runners pay careful attention to their mental and physical health and agility, their diet, their equipment (shoes, clothing, technology), and the way they spend their time. Runners are attentive to and routinely engaged in disciplined practices that enable them to run well (maintaining a rigorous diet, adhering to a schedule, etc.).

In the same way, I want to suggest that there's a relevant difference between the momentary activity of thinking philosophically and living a philosophical kind of life. Just as there's a crucial difference between the momentary activity of *running to win a race* and *being a runner*, there's also a crucial difference between *philosophizing for a course grade* and *living philosophically*.

It may surprise you to learn that philosophy did not always have the public relations problem that it has today. There's a much older tradition in which philosophy was viewed as intimately tied to the everyday rhythms of one's life, as an all-encompassing life-posture that enables humans to see the world as it really is and to orient themselves to it *for the sake of living well*. For ancient Greek and Roman thinkers such as Plato, Aristotle, Epicurus, and Seneca, philosophical activity is not a momentary activity one happens to engage in every so often, like attending an occasional lecture or reading and thinking about a complex philosophical issue. Rather, for these thinkers and many of their disciples, the person whose life is devoted to the love and pursuit of wisdom (the person who lives *the philosophical kind of life*) is more like the person whose life is marked by the activities of writing, playing, practicing, and teaching music (living *the musical kind of life*) than like the person who owns an instrument and happens to dust it off and play it every now and then.

In contemporary philosophy, this more ancient conception of philosophy as a way of life has been unpacked most clearly and extensively in the works of French philosopher Pierre Hadot (1922–2010) and the late American philosopher John Cooper (1939–2022).[1] In

---

1. See Hadot, *What Is Ancient Philosophy?*; Hadot, *Philosophy as a Way of Life*; Cooper, *Pursuits of Wisdom*. See also Nussbaum, *Therapy of Desire*.

careful historical detail, Hadot and Cooper have each shown that a more ancient conception of the philosophical life involved an entire life-orientation, a *way of being in the world*, aimed at the art of living well.

According to Hadot and Cooper, for the ancients, philosophy was not confined to the halls of the academy, as it is normally understood to be today. Rather, philosophy permeates and informs every aspect of an individual's life. As Cooper puts it, philosophy is the captain or "steerman of one's whole life," and not some purely abstract intellectual exercise.[2] Philosophy, Hadot claims, "appears in its original aspect: not as a theoretical construct, but as a *method for training people to live and look at the world in a new way*. It is an attempt to transform mankind."[3] For ancient philosophers, both Christian and non-Christian, philosophy's chief aim is to help one structure one's life to properly see and orient oneself to the world, ultimately for the sake of living well. Philosophy, in the words of the Roman Stoic philosopher Seneca (4 BC–AD 65), "tells us how to live, not how to talk."[4]

Scholars of classical and medieval philosophy have pointed out that older thinkers such as Socrates, Plato, Aristotle, Epicurus, Epictetus, Seneca, Marcus Aurelius, Cicero, Boethius, and Hugh of Saint Victor understood philosophy first and foremost as *therapeutic*. Philosophy was a kind of *care or therapy of the soul*, not in the thin, modern sense of making you feel better about yourself but in the older, thicker sense of promoting the *objective health of the soul*.[5]

2. Cooper, *Pursuits of Wisdom*, 7.
3. Hadot, *Philosophy as a Way of Life*, 10 (emphasis added).
4. Seneca, *Moral Epistles to Lucilius* 20.2, quoted in Sharpe and Ure, *Philosophy as a Way of Life*, 76.
5. See Hadot, *What Is Ancient Philosophy?*; Hadot, *Philosophy as a Way of Life*; Cooper, *Pursuits of Wisdom*. See also Nussbaum, *Therapy of Desire*. For a helpful overview of this aspect of ancient and medieval philosophy, see Sharpe and Ure, *Philosophy as a Way of Life*, 53.

Along these lines, Epicurus (341–270 BC) famously said, "Just as there is no profit in medicine if it does not expel the diseases of the body, so there is no profit in philosophy either, if it does not expel the suffering of the mind."[6]

But what exactly is the suffering of the mind that requires healing, we might ask? In contrast to Christian moral teaching found in Scripture, Hellenistic and Roman philosophers had no explicit doctrine of the powerful sin dynamics that can disintegrate and spoil a human life (Rom. 7; Eph. 4:22–24; 1 Pet. 2:11; 2 Pet. 1:4). Rather, the type of healing they have in mind involves achieving a greater peace and inner freedom from the suffering that comes in the wake of unruly and unwanted desires.

Each ancient school's prescribed course of philosophical therapy— whether Platonic, Epicurean, Stoic, or whatever—was geared toward taming unruly and unwanted desires, desires that are either baseless (such as excessive fear of things outside one's control) or unsatisfied (such as desire for more influence, power, or money). In the *Apology*, Socrates repeatedly calls out his dialogue partners, asking, "Are you not ashamed of your eagerness to possess as much wealth, reputation, and honors as possible, while you do not care for nor give thought to wisdom or truth, or the best possible state of your soul?"[7] In fact, Socrates sums up his own philosophical therapeutics when he says, "For I go around doing nothing but persuading both young and old among you not to care for your body or your wealth in preference to or as strongly as for the best possible state of your souls."[8] This same therapeutic element of ancient philosophy is underscored nicely by Seneca: "'If you are studying philosophy, it is well.' For this is just what 'being well' means. Without philosophy the mind is sickly, and

---

6. Epicurus, *Selected Fragments* 221, quoted in Sharpe and Ure, *Philosophy as a Way of Life*, 53.

7. *Apology* 29d–e, in Plato, *Trial and Death of Socrates*, 32.

8. *Apology* 30a–b, in Plato, *Trial and Death of Socrates*, 32–33.

the body, too, though it may be very powerful, is strong only as that of a madman or a lunatic is strong."[9] This therapeutic emphasis is so prominent to an ancient philosophical way of life that Martha Nussbaum, an expert in ancient Greek and Roman philosophy, has labeled it the "medical model of philosophizing."[10]

The Philosophical Way of Life as the Purely Reason-Driven Life?

There is, however, one important way in which Hadot's and Cooper's accounts of philosophy as a way of life in antiquity diverge. This divergence has to do with whether the ancients thought that the use of reason alone was sufficient to live a distinctively philosophical way of life. Hadot answers in the negative, Cooper in the affirmative.

Let's take a closer look, starting with Hadot. According to Hadot, the center of philosophy as a way of life in antiquity involved distinctively *spiritual exercises*[11] that were aimed at the spiritual and moral transformation of the individual. Indeed, Hadot goes so far as to say that "it is *philosophy itself* that the ancients thought of as spiritual exercise,"[12] and "to the same extent that the philosophical life is equivalent to the practice of spiritual exercises . . . it is a conversion, a total transformation of one's vision, life-style, and behavior."[13]

9. Seneca, *Moral Epistles to Lucilius* 15.1, quoted in Sharpe and Ure, *Philosophy as a Way of Life*, 85.

10. Nussbaum, *Therapy of Desire*, 3–4. See also Frede, *Essays in Ancient Philosophy*, 225.

11. Hadot recognizes the unease many contemporary philosophers have with the term "spiritual" exercises. Nevertheless, he thinks such a term is necessary to capture the role these exercises played in antiquity in shaping and forming the soul. See Hadot, *Philosophy as a Way of Life*, 81–82. Hadot also points out that the later Christian reception of the spiritual exercises is evidenced by Saint Ignatius of Loyola's *Spiritual Exercises*.

12. Hadot, *Philosophy as a Way of Life*, 126.

13. Hadot, *Philosophy as a Way of Life*, 103.

According to this more expansive view of philosophy as a way of life in antiquity, the philosophical life includes both rational apprehension and the disciplined practice of action-oriented, spiritual exercises designed to make the practitioner's soul fit for properly *seeing* what is true, *loving* what is good, and *navigating* life accordingly. These exercises aim at tuning the practitioner both to discern the right chords on the right musical score of life and to play that music in a beautiful, harmonic way.

In general, the spiritual exercises were viewed by the ancients as a way to train and sculpt the soul (*psyche*), a practice they referred to as *askesis*. Spiritual exercises were thus similar to physical exercises, which were viewed as a way to train and sculpt (*askesis*) the physical body. Hadot remarks that "just as, by dint of repeated physical exercises, athletes give new form and strength to their bodies, so the philosopher develops his strength of soul, modifies his inner climate, transforms his vision of the world, and, finally, his entire being."[14] It was the personal transformation of the practitioner—mind, will, and desire—by way of soul training or *askesis* that was the overarching purpose of the spiritual exercises. In short, according to Hadot, tuning or training the soul by way of the spiritual exercises was an essential aspect of philosophical therapeutics, designed to bring about a greater strength and health of soul, "a profound transformation of the individual's mode of seeing and being."[15]

This therapeutic training (*askesis*) of the soul to make it healthy enough to see the true and love the good involved both individual exercises (such as meditation, therapy of the passions, attention, self-examination, research, thorough investigation, listening, and memorization) and communal exercises (such as friendship and Socratic dialogue).[16]

14. Hadot, *Philosophy as a Way of Life*, 102.
15. Hadot, *Philosophy as a Way of Life*, 83.
16. For two important classical sources on friendship and its vital importance to a philosophical way of life, see Plutarch, *Moralia*, 45–69; Cicero, *On Old Age*, 103–213.

Here is a representative sample of some of the most significant spiritual exercises practiced in antiquity,[17] several of which we'll take a closer look at in the next chapter:

- reading
- research
- thorough investigation
- attention
- listening
- memorization
- Socratic dialogue

- friendship
- self-examination
- therapy of the passions ("self-mastery")
- meditation (on the present moment, on death)

As you can see from this sample list, some spiritual exercises emphasize the training of the *mind* (reading, research, thorough investigation, memorization, Socratic dialogue, attention), some emphasize the training of the *passions* or *desires* (therapy of the passions or self-mastery), and some emphasize a blended mixture of the two (meditation, self-examination, friendship, listening).

According to Hadot, all the ancient philosophical schools in Athens, such as Plato's Academy (387 BC), Aristotle's Lyceum (334 BC), Epicurus's Garden (late fourth century BC), and Zeno's Porch (late fourth century BC), incorporated similar spiritual practices into the Platonic, Aristotelian, Epicurean, and Stoic ways of life, respectively. In summary, then, according to Hadot's more expansive reading of an ancient philosophical way of life, "The philosophical act is not situated merely on the cognitive level, but on that of the self and of being. . . . It is a conversion which turns our entire life upside down, changing the life of the person who goes through it."[18]

17. As Hadot points out, there are two largely overlapping lists of spiritual exercises that have survived to this day, both from the Jewish Hellenistic thinker Philo of Alexandria. For an extended discussion of these exercises, see Hadot, *Philosophy as a Way of Life*, 84.
18. Hadot, *Philosophy as a Way of Life*, 83.

In sharp contrast to Hadot, John Cooper has argued that the spiritual exercises, so understood, had no significant place in ancient philosophical ways of life. By Cooper's lights, Hadot's focus on transformative exercises or "spiritual gymnastics" as essential to the ancient philosophical way of life is misguided and distorts the ancient philosophical tradition. Instead, Cooper argues that the ancient philosophical way of life was the *purely reason-driven life* and made no use of spiritually transformative exercises.[19] The only kind of philosophical therapeutics that contribute to the health of the soul are activities that strengthen one's rational and cognitive grasp on the world.

Let's call Cooper's view, that the philosophical way of life is the purely reason-driven life, *intellectualism.* Cooper elaborates on his purely reason-driven understanding of ancient philosophy as a way of life in the following passage: "For these thinkers, *only reason*, and what reason could discover and establish as the truth, could be an ultimately acceptable basis on which to live a life—and for them philosophy is *nothing more*, but also nothing less, than the art or discipline that develops and perfects the human capacity of reason."[20] Intellectualism, I believe, is what comes to most people's minds when they hear the word "philosophy" or the phrase "living philosophically." But pause to note how strong this purely reason-driven conception of philosophy as a way of life is: unless you can explicitly reason to and defend your core beliefs about reality and the good life, you cannot be said to be living philosophically.

Why the Philosophical Life Is Not the Purely Reason-Driven Life

As you can no doubt see, intellectualism sets a very high bar for the prospects of living philosophically, both for the ancients and

19. I owe the phrase "purely reason-driven life" to Grimm and Cohoe, "What Is Philosophy as a Way of Life?"

20. Cooper, *Pursuits of Wisdom*, 6 (emphasis added). For this quotation, I am indebted to Grimm and Cohoe, "What Is Philosophy as a Way of Life?"

for us. Since I am not a historian of ancient philosophy, I'll set aside Cooper's strictly historical claim that ancient philosophy itself is best understood along intellectualist lines.[21] My sole aim here will be to evaluate Cooper's optimism that intellectualism remains a viable view of the philosophical life today and his view that we too should view the philosophical way of life as the purely reason-driven life.

In my estimation, the price of intellectualism is simply too high; its vices far outweigh its virtues. Thus, I don't think intellectualism is true. And you shouldn't either—or so I'll argue. I'll offer three reasons for siding with Hadot and viewing philosophy as a way of life expansive enough to include the spiritual exercises and thus as more than merely "strengthening one's rational grasp of truths."[22]

First and foremost, the Bible and the wider Christian tradition bear witness that the *kind of person you are*—including your deep-seated loves, desires, and motivations—can either directly *help* or directly *hinder* your ability to properly see reality and thus to fit your life into it. Scripture teaches that it is the pure in heart who will see God (Matt. 5:8) and that we are to "strive for . . . the holiness without which no one will see the Lord" (Heb. 12:14). On the flip side, a disordered moral condition of the heart warps the shape of the mind and twists its natural function. The minds of those whose loves are disordered and turned inward are given over to futility and "ignorance . . . due to their hardness of heart" (Eph. 4:18). And, insofar as Christian spiritual practices (fasting, silence, solitude, meditation, prayer, etc.) are aimed at the transformation of the entire person in dependence on the Holy Spirit, they can help cultivate the right moral and spiritual preconditions for properly aligning the intellect with reality.

---

21. For a more thorough critique of Cooper's historical claim, see Grimm and Cohoe, "What Is Philosophy as a Way of Life?"
22. Cooper, "Ancient Philosophy as a Way of Life," 40.

In fact, the idea that our desires and appetites need to first be trained to properly see and grasp truth and live in accordance with it is found even in ancient thinkers such as Plato and Aristotle. In the *Republic*, Plato recommends that music and physical training be used to make reason and spirit (*thumos*, one of the nonrational parts of the human soul for Plato) "concordant"—meaning that they work in tandem, thereby allowing reason to take up its proper role as the main pilot of human life.[23] Elsewhere, in the *Timaeus*, Plato says that "there is one deliverance from both [madness and ignorance]: neither to exercise the soul without exercising the body, nor the body without the soul, so that, aiding one another, they become equally balanced and sound. Thus, the student of mathematics or some other discipline who works with exceeding care for his power of thought must also provide exercise for his body, by attending to physical training, while the one carefully molding his body must repay his soul with exercises, making use of music and every pursuit of wisdom (*philosophiai*)."[24]

As philosophers Caleb Cohoe and Stephen Grimm point out, an implication of taking what Plato says in the *Republic* and what he says in the *Timaeus* together is that Plato believed that without music and bodily training ordering the nonrational parts of the soul, reason would not be able to function properly and thus would not clearly perceive what is true and good.[25] Thus, even for Plato, "Using our reason well requires the proper preparatory exercises of both body and soul."[26] This is a far cry from the purely reason-driven life of intellectualism.

---

23. See *Republic* 441e–442a, in *Plato: Complete Works*, 1073. I owe this point to Grimm and Cohoe, "What Is Philosophy as a Way of Life?," 239.

24. Plato, *Timaeus* 88b–c, quoted in (and translated by) Grimm and Cohoe, "What Is Philosophy as a Way of Life?," 240.

25. Grimm and Cohoe, "What Is Philosophy as a Way of Life?," 240.

26. Grimm and Cohoe, "What Is Philosophy as a Way of Life?," 240.

In addition, this very tight connection between the kind of person you are and your ability to intellectually attune yourself to reality—particularly the reality and nature of the supreme and highest good, the triune God—was a common theme among the early church fathers, Eastern and Western. The great Eastern church father Gregory Nazianzen (329–390) famously said, "Not to everyone, my friends, does it belong to philosophize about God. . . . It is permitted only to those who have been examined, and are passed masters in meditation, and who have been previously purified in soul and body, or at the very least are being purified." According to Gregory, grave moral and intellectual dangers await those who rashly attempt to wade into "the depths of God" (1 Cor. 2:10) without the buoyancy of character required for the right use of reason concerning divine matters. "For the impure to touch the pure is, we may safely say, not safe, just as it is unsafe to fix weak eyes upon the sun's rays."[27]

In the very same vein, Augustine (354–430) remarked that God "can only be discerned by minds that are wholly purified, and that they themselves [the spiritually immature] are unable to see or to comprehend it for this reason, because the weak eye of the human mind cannot be fixed on a light so dazzling, unless it has been nourished and become stronger by the justice of faith."[28] We find this same emphasis—that is, on the tight connection between the moral condition of one's soul and the ability of the mind to clearly see and function properly—throughout patristic, medieval, Reformation, and post-Reformation Christian thought.

A second worry about an intellectualist view of the philosophical way of life is that it is overly elitist and exclusive. It is elitist insofar as it seems to reduce the philosophical way of life to the life of academic

27. Gregory Nazianzen, "Select Orations," 285.
28. Augustine, *Trinity*, 7. I owe this reference to Jamieson and Wittman, *Biblical Reasoning*.

or argumentative discourse; *only* those who have "argued through, rationally worked out, rationally grasped and rationally defended" their core beliefs can truly live the philosophical kind of life.[29] But this strikes me—even as one who makes an honest wage on academic and argumentative discourse—as far too narrow and rigid at best and predicated on an overly one-dimensional, reason-heavy view of the human being at worst.

Intellectualism excludes philosophical novices, those who are not yet able to thoroughly reason to and rationally defend their core beliefs, since they cannot live the purely reason-driven life, according to Cooper. This needlessly restricts the philosophical life to seasoned philosophical veterans and bars newly enlisted philosophical recruits. But if one can live a musical or an athletic way of life and still be a musical or athletic novice, why can't one also do this when it comes to living a philosophical way of life?[30]

A third worry with intellectualism is that it is overly individualistic. As Cohoe and Grimm point out, Cooper's "language suggests that ancient philosophy operated via atomistic individuals deciding which schools to endorse on the basis of abstract arguments, which neglects the social aspects of philosophical formation."[31] And, as we've already seen, friendship, spiritual guidance (between master and disciple), and Socratic dialogue were all understood by the ancients as important communal spiritual exercises that contributed to the health and integrity of the soul.

If there are problems with viewing the philosophical life as nothing more than the purely reason-driven life, what might a more modest, inclusive, "working-class" view of philosophy as a way of life look

---

29. Cooper, "Ancient Philosophy as a Way of Life," 17, quoted in Grimm and Cohoe, "What Is Philosophy as a Way of Life?," 245.
30. This point is helpfully articulated in Cohoe and Grimm, "What It Takes to Live Philosophically."
31. Cohoe and Grimm, "What It Takes to Live Philosophically."

like? Well, for one, it would involve a significantly broader understanding of the philosophical enterprise, in terms of both its nature and its scope. In terms of its nature, a more modest approach can and should expand the philosophical enterprise beyond formal, argumentative reasoning reserved for the highly educated and the razor-sharp intellectuals among us. In terms of its scope, the philosophical life extends beyond the college curriculum and weaves its way into the mundane, ordinary rhythms of human life.

This more inclusive understanding of philosophy as a way of life is captured well by Plutarch (AD 45–120), a Greek philosopher influenced by Plato, in reference to Socrates himself:

> Most people imagine that philosophy consists in delivering discourses from the heights of a chair, and in giving classes based on texts. But what these people utterly miss is the uninterrupted philosophy which we see being practiced every day in a way which is perfectly equal to itself. . . . Socrates did not set up grandstands for his audience and did not sit upon a professorial chair; he had no fixed timetable for talking or walking with his friends. Rather, he did philosophy sometimes by joking with them, and finally by going to prison and drinking poison. He was the first to show that at all times and in every place, everything that happens to us, daily life gives us the opportunity to do philosophy.[32]

According to this more modest understanding of the philosophical way of life, philosophy "is something we are all doing all the time, a continuous, background activity which is likely to go badly if we don't attend to it."[33]

---

32. Plutarch, *Whether a Man Should Engage in Politics When He Is Old*, quoted in Hadot, *What Is Ancient Philosophy?*, 38.
33. Mary Midgley, *What Is Philosophy For?*, quoted in McPherson, *Virtue and Meaning*, 168.

How to Live Philosophically

Let's now try to get crystal clear what this more expansive, "working-class" view of the philosophical life involves. Specifically, what conditions set this way of life apart from others such as the musical or the athletic ways of life? If we move away from intellectualism and bring spiritual practices into the orbit of what it means to live philosophically, what is it that makes this way of life distinctively *philosophical*? Here I will focus on what it means to live philosophically in a general way, and then in the next chapter I will discuss what it might mean to live a distinctively *Christian* philosophical life.

Reflecting on this older conception of philosophy as a way of life, Cohoe and Grimm offer three conditions concerning what it means to live the philosophical way of life:

1. *Commit to an existential map*: Practitioners of a philosophical way of life are committed to an existential map that specifies what truly *is* and what *ought to be*.

2. *Orient your life around it*: Practitioners of a philosophical way of life have their life and practices structured by the existential map to which they are committed.

3. *Engage in truth-directed practices*: The life and everyday practices of practitioners of a philosophical way of life are aimed at truth and responsive to evidence.[34]

According to condition 1, practitioners of a distinctively *philosophical* way of life reflectively commit to an encompassing "world-picture" or existential map of reality that carries with it visions about what is *real* and what is *good* and ought to be pursued (value-prescribing). To live

---

34. These have been adapted from Cohoe and Grimm, "What It Takes to Live Philosophically." Cohoe and Grimm do not use the phrase "existential map."

philosophically, then, you have to be reflective to some degree—and thus aware of the basic contours and reasons for and against competing visions of reality and the good life. This is precisely why Socrates called the philosophical life "the examined life." Because humans are meaning-seeking animals, we are naturally moved by wonder and awe at the world and its intricate contours, which then brings us to ponder the meaning of it all and how it all hangs together. The philosophical life, then, is the life that is in intellectual gear to some degree—whether first, second, third, fourth, or fifth gear—and not idling in intellectual neutral. And, in the end, whichever existential map our experiences of wonder and sustained reflection lead us to commit to will inevitably guide how we navigate and direct our lives.

As for condition 2, practitioners of a distinctively philosophical way of life will not only intellectually commit themselves to a particular vision of reality and the good life; *they will also structure their lives around this vision.* The steady rhythms of their lives—who they are and what they do (what they devote their time, resources, and energies to)—will be informed by and anchored in their particular vision of reality and the good life, in the same way that the lives of musicians are structured around the activities distinctive of the musical kind of life (writing music, playing music, practicing music, listening to music, and teaching music).

It is important to point out that the fulfillment of this second condition for living philosophically more often than not comes in degrees; one's life can be *more* or *less* structured around one's vision of reality and the good life. Cohoe and Grimm illustrate this by using the example of someone who is committed to the value and importance of bodily health. Structuring one's life in accordance with a commitment to bodily health is consistent with a range of lifestyles and practices, including the lifestyle and daily practices of the bodybuilder and fitness guru, at one extreme of the spectrum, and the lifestyle and daily practices of the person who is just beginning to take up physical exercise, at the other end of the spectrum. Both individuals structure their lives around the good of bodily health, but to very different degrees.

The same holds true when it comes to living philosophically. Consider a first-year college student who has just begun the quest of making meaningful sense of reality as a whole, as well as a professional philosopher who writes and teaches philosophy for a living. Both individuals have chosen to structure their lives around philosophizing, and both of their lives count equally as philosophical in the sense described in condition 2. Thus, according to condition 2, you don't need to be a philosophy major or occupy an endowed academic chair to live philosophically.

Finally, let's explore condition 3, concerning what it means to live philosophically: the life and everyday practices of practitioners of a philosophical way of life need to be both aimed at truth and responsive to evidence. This last condition has two aspects.

The first aspect pertains to how one is postured in the world, whether one's everyday life and everyday practice leans *into* or *away from* a healthy love, pursuit, and reception of the truth. Practitioners of philosophy as a way of life are *truth-sensitive*, we might say, and it shows in the way they conduct their everyday lives.

The second aspect of condition 3 involves the *way* in which one pursues truth, how one goes about seeking what is true and what makes up the good life. Those who live philosophically are *reasons-sensitive*, and it shows in the way they conduct their everyday lives. They strive to be the kind of people who are receptive to evidence for and against their chosen existential map of reality and the good life. And precisely because they love and actively hunger for truth, people who live philosophically will be increasingly marked by various intellectual virtues, including intellectual attentiveness, humility, courage, charity, and open-mindedness, even in the face of great risk and harm. (Just consider the outcome of Socrates's life, described in Plato's

Apology). So, if your closest friend tells you that they've begun to pursue a philosophical way of life and then proceeds to tell you that they spend every waking moment watching sports or that they read books or listen to podcasts only from thinkers on their end of the ideological spectrum, then their life is not marked by truth-aimed activities and thus is not a *philosophical* way of life.

If we adopt Hadot's more expansive view of the philosophical way of life, fulfilling both aspects of this third condition will inevitably involve the regular practice of various truth-aimed spiritual exercises—meditation, self-examination, attention, reading, therapy of the passions, and so forth. These exercises are "truth-aimed" (in the sense outlined in condition 3) precisely because they ready the soul to better *see* and *respond* to the world as it really is, for the sake of living well. They help fashion us into the kind of people who are *apt* to make contact with the way the world is (truth) and to be responsive and open to correction when our vision of reality is distorted (as it will inevitably be at some point).

But what might a distinctively Christian philosophical way of life look like? It is to this question that we now turn.

4

Recovering Christian Philosophy as a Way of Life

We have seen that many ancient thinkers, both Christian and non-Christian, viewed philosophy as an all-encompassing life-posture that was therapeutic in that it aimed at the objective health of the human soul rather than at the merely theoretical use of reason. This is what one notable author has called the "medical model of philosophizing."[1] But since many today do not naturally conceive of Christian philosophy along these lines, it may be helpful to provide a detailed example from the Christian tradition of the therapeutic value of philosophy. Get ready: we're about to get positively medieval.

Boethius on Lady Philosophy's Therapeutics

One of the most influential examples of the medical model of philosophizing in the Christian tradition (and of the therapeutic value

---

1. Nussbaum, *Therapy of Desire*, 3–4. See also Frede, *Essays in Ancient Philosophy*, 225.

of philosophy more generally) is found in the work *The Consolation of Philosophy*, written by a sixth-century Roman Christian philosopher named Anicius Manlius Severinus Boethius.[2] Boethius lived from approximately 480 to 524 and was a man who stood at "the crossroads of the Classical and Medieval worlds."[3] He was a fascinating and learned Christian thinker whose life and writings would come to have a significant impact on later developments in Christian theology and philosophy up through the Middle Ages as well as on many more-modern Christian thinkers such as C. S. Lewis.[4] Boethius was from a rather well-off Roman aristocratic family and served in several powerful Roman political positions during his life. He even served as one of the most important advisers to the Ostrogothic king Theodoric, the first barbarian king of Italy.

The setting of Boethius's *Consolation* is a jail cell where the narrator is awaiting his execution. But this setting is no mere fictional embellishment; it is autobiography. When the *Consolation* was written, Boethius himself was in exile, imprisoned and awaiting execution at the hands of King Theodoric (whom he had formerly advised).

The *Consolation* begins with a detailed description of the prisoner's sickly physical and spiritual condition. The prisoner is described as spiritually ill, one who is "in deep despair" and whose "sight grows dim."[5] Though he previously possessed a bright and hungry mind, ready and able to explore nature's hidden causes and explanations, there is now only darkness, heaviness, and the ability "to contemplate the lowly dust."[6] The prisoner suffers from a loss of existential clarity and sight, we might say; he can no longer see the world as it is—that is, with full moral clarity.

---

2. In this section I am indebted to Philips, "Lady Philosophy's Therapeutic Method."
3. Victor Watts, introduction to Boethius, *Consolation of Philosophy*, xi.
4. See Lewis, *Discarded Image*, 75–79.
5. Boethius, *Consolation of Philosophy* 1.2, p. 5.
6. Boethius, *Consolation of Philosophy* 1.2, p. 6.

In the narrator's dire and sickly state, a woman of radiance, vitality, stature, and timeworn wisdom—Lady Philosophy—comes to his aid. Lady Philosophy is Boethius's literary personification of philosophy. In contrast to the narrator's pitiful and blinded state, Lady Philosophy is described as of "awe-inspiring appearance, her eyes burning and keen beyond the usual power of men." Her stature is towering, and her clothes are made of "imperishable material." Lady Philosophy is described as ancient and full of years, yet she still "possessed a vivid color and undiminished vigor." But even in her radiance, she has been unduly neglected, like a beautiful "statue covered in dust."[7]

Before the sickly narrator can even recognize the true identity of Lady Philosophy, she diagnoses him as suffering from a kind of life-threatening "lethargy" or drowsiness of the mind, a type of existential disorientation that will prove deadly if not properly treated. According to Lady Philosophy, the narrator is suffering from a type of amnesia or forgetfulness: he has "forgotten for a while who he is, but he will soon remember once he has recognized me."[8]

As several scholars have insightfully pointed out, both in his depiction of Lady Philosophy as a wise physician and in the details surrounding her diagnosis of "lethargy," Boethius shows he was well aware of the medical literature of his time.[9] When Boethius depicts Lady Philosophy as a competent physician who is able to diagnose and care for the sickly condition of the narrator's soul, he is likely drawing on some of the most influential medical literature of the Greco-Roman period, including the writings of Galen (AD 129–216) and the later work of influential Roman medical writer Caelius Aurelianus (likely fifth century).

---

7. Boethius, *Consolation of Philosophy* 1.1, p. 4.
8. Boethius, *Consolation of Philosophy* 1.2, p. 6.
9. See Schmid, "Boethius and the Claims of Philosophy."

Regarding the idea of the physician as philosopher (and the philosopher as physician), Boethius more likely than not had an eye on Galen. Galen, in his little work titled "That the Best Doctor Is Also a Philosopher," stated that "clearly all true doctors must also be philosophers." He thought that physicians should strive to cultivate intellectual and moral virtue by way of philosophical reflection so that they can "employ their art in the right way."[10] To his fellow physicians who would carry the mantle of Hippocrates (460–375 BC)—widely considered to be the father of medicine—Galen gave the following charge: "We must, then, practice philosophy, if we are true followers of Hippocrates."[11] Boethius was aware of Galen's work, including the idea that physicians should be philosophers and the ancient medical model of philosophizing.

For Lady Philosophy's specific diagnosis of "lethargy," Boethius is likely indebted to Caelius Aurelianus's explanation of the symptoms and proper treatment of the medical condition of lethargy, outlined in book 2 ("De lethargo") of his work *On Acute Diseases*. Caelius said of lethargy that it "receives its name from the loss of memory which the disease involves" and that the name comes from "the Greek word for forgetfulness and for idleness."[12] According to Caelius, lethargy involved several key physical and psychological symptoms, including acute fever, heaviness of body, tiredness, depression, and a mental daze and dullness of the senses.

With this Greco-Roman medical tradition in mind, Boethius has Lady Philosophy play the role of soul physician who accurately diagnoses the narrator's lethargic condition and prescribes the right course of treatment for it. Lady Philosophy pinpoints three interrelated root causes of the narrator's dullness of sight and existential

10. *Galen: Selected Works*, 33.
11. *Galen: Selected Works*, 34.
12. Caelius Aurelianus, *On Acute Diseases*, quoted in Philips, "Lady Philosophy's Therapeutic Method."

disorientation: he has been lured away by false visions of (1) his true nature, (2) the nature of the good life, and (3) the nature of reality itself. All of these involve his failure to see the world in its proper light and to rightly orient himself to it.[13]

Owing to the seriousness of the narrator's existential disorientation and blindness, and in line with common medical practices of the day, Lady Philosophy's course of therapy or treatment involves both gentler and stronger remedies. She first prescribes "gentler medicines" with the hope that "the ever treacherous passions may be dispelled, and you will be able to see the resplendent light of truth." Then, and only then, will the prisoner be stable and healthy enough to receive the stronger, sharper medicines to come.[14]

Lady Philosophy's gentler remedies consist in a series of short, rhetorical insights designed to help the prisoner see that the things taken from him (wealth, power, physical freedom, social and political influence) were never really his to begin with and were, in themselves, never capable of delivering on their empty promises of lasting joy and ultimate happiness. Since each of these goods rise and fall with the ever-changing tides of circumstance, they can never bring ultimate and lasting rest to the human soul. By contrast, the weightiest, most stable, and most enduring goods in human life can never be taken from him and thus are immune to circumstances beyond his control.

These initial, gentler remedies help strengthen the patient to handle the stronger remedies to come; they stabilize him enough to receive a more potent course of treatment. The stronger or sharper remedies administered by Lady Philosophy include a series of detailed philosophical explorations and dialogues that aim first to remind the patient what ultimate happiness is *not*[15] and then to demonstrate what ultimate

---

13. Boethius, *Consolation of Philosophy* 1.6, pp. 19–20.
14. Boethius, *Consolation of Philosophy* 1.5, p. 18.
15. See Boethius, *Consolation of Philosophy* 2.5, 3.1–9 for descriptions of what happiness is not.

happiness *is* and how he must look beyond the creaturely realm to trace it back to its true source: God himself as the "Author of all health."[16]

Lady Philosophy argues, in line with much classical moral philosophy, that the greatest and highest good for humans must, once obtained, "leave nothing more to be desired"[17] and thus must be fully sufficient *in itself*. The idea here is this: We don't desire a flourishing and happy life *for the sake of something else*. Rather, we desire such a life *for its own sake*. The truly flourishing human life—the abundant life that Jesus speaks of—is that which leads us to a place of enduring and stable rest (Matt. 11:28–30; John 10:10; Ps. 23).

According to Lady Philosophy, if you devote your life to the abundance of possessions, wealth, power, social influence, and so forth, you will never have enough and will forever remain unsatisfied. Lady Philosophy is at pains to remind the prisoner that these are "shadows of happiness"[18] and "sidetracks" that "cannot bring us to the destination they promise."[19] Lady Philosophy, and philosophical reflection in general, administers the remedy that ultimately enables the prisoner to turn his "gaze in a different direction and recognize the pattern of true happiness."[20] And, in true classical Christian fashion, Lady Philosophy concludes her stronger therapeutic remedies with a potent dose of reality: the kind of rich happiness that leaves nothing more to be desired and that each of us ultimately yearns for can be found only in God himself.

A Closer Look at a *Christian* Philosophical Way of Life

Our brief journey with Boethius and Lady Philosophy illustrates that the notion of Christian philosophy as a way of life that is medicinal

---

16. Boethius, *Consolation of Philosophy* 1.6, p. 20.
17. Boethius, *Consolation of Philosophy* 3.2, p. 48.
18. Boethius, *Consolation of Philosophy* 3.1, p. 47.
19. Boethius, *Consolation of Philosophy* 3.8, p. 60.
20. Boethius, *Consolation of Philosophy* 3.1, p. 47.

and therapeutic for the human condition is no stranger to the Christian tradition. But can we clarify just what the Christian philosophical way of life amounts to? I think we can.

So let's begin to apply the three conditions concerning what it means to live philosophically (see chap. 3) to the question of what it means to live a *Christian philosophical way of life* (CPWL) in particular:

1. *Commit to an existential map shaped by the Christian story*: Practitioners of a CPWL are committed to "the faith that was once for all delivered to the saints" (Jude 3) as the existential map that specifies what truly *is* and what *ought to be*.

2. *Orient your life around a Christian existential map*: Practitioners of a CPWL have their life and everyday practices oriented around the vision of reality and the good life shaped by the Christian story.

3. *Engage in grace-empowered, truth-directed practices*: The life and everyday practices of practitioners of a CPWL are grace-empowered, aimed at truth, and responsive to evidence.

Let's start with condition 1 concerning how to live a Christian philosophical way of life. The Christian philosophical life is committed to an existential map that is referred to in Scripture as "the faith that was once for all delivered to the saints" (Jude 3), "the mysteries of God" (1 Cor. 4:1), and "the good deposit" of faith that has been passed down through the teaching of Jesus and the apostles (2 Tim. 1:14). What exactly does this "good deposit" include in terms of philosophical content? Quite a bit, actually.

Let's briefly unpack what I take to be three of the most important coordinates on any existential map[21] and see how each of them is filled in by the Christian story:

---

21. These three coordinates are inspired by and slightly adapted from Willard, *Knowing Christ Today*, 45–50.

- *The reality question*: What is real?
- *The good-life question*: Who is a truly good person? What is a truly good life?
- *The character-formation question*: How does one become a truly good person?

These three questions are perennial philosophical questions that have occupied the attention of humanity's most formidable minds—Plato, Aristotle, Augustine, Boethius, Anselm, Aquinas, Locke, Hume, Kant, Kierkegaard, Nietzsche, and others.

According to the Christian story, *the reality question* finds its answer in the triune God and the creative effects of his free and gracious initiative. God alone is rock-bottom, fundamental, and fully alive in himself (Exod. 3:14); everything else borrows its existence from God at each moment (Acts 17:24–26; Rev. 4:11). The triune God is the creative origin and source of created existence; there is God, and then there is everything else. The triune God is "before all things" (Col. 1:17). God has no rival, God has no equal, for "from him and through him and to him are all things" (Rom. 11:36). God is due North of the true and most satisfying existential map of reality. All other creaturely coordinates are *from* him and *for* him and find their proper place in right relation to him.

Let's turn briefly to how the Christian story answers *the good-life question*: who is a truly good person, and what is a truly good life? At bottom, the truly good person is anyone who currently enjoys an eternal kind of life, anyone who is presently alive in the kingdom of God (John 17:3). The one who is truly well off is the one who *knows* God in the richest and fullest sense of the word: that is, "anyone who is interactively engaged with God and with the various dynamic dimensions of his reigning." And to be alive in the kingdom of the triune God, who is the source and standard of supreme love, is to be saturated with love for God and others. A truly good life, then, is any life that "is pervaded with love: love for the God who 'first loved us' and who in his Son taught us what love is (1 John 4:7–12)."[22]

The person who has "made it" in life, we might say, is not the person who has acquired the most possessions (Luke 12:15) or landed the highest-paying job. It is not the person who has the largest social media platform, who is the best educated, or who pastors the largest church in the area. And so on and so on. Rather, the person who is interactively related to God and marked by the kind of selfless love in which God delights is the one who is truly worthy to be admired and emulated (Jer. 9:23–24).

Finally, let's turn to *the character-formation question*. According to the teaching of Jesus, you become the kind of person you truly *ought* to be by, first and foremost, placing your confidence in Jesus Christ and becoming his daily apprentice in kingdom living. We learn to live the truly good and fulfilling life not by sitting at the feet of wealthy entrepreneurs, savvy politicians, tech gurus, social media giants, celebrities, or Ivy League university professors. We cannot become truly good merely by signaling to others that we care about justice, by downloading the latest flashy app, or by upgrading to the most recent software or hardware.

Rather, as recorded in Matthew 11:29, Jesus tells us how to find the soul-satisfying rest for which we were created: "Take my yoke upon you, and learn from me, for I am gentle and lowly in heart, and you will find rest for your souls." As Christian philosopher Dallas Willard has demonstrated so well over the years, discipleship is daily apprenticing yourself to Jesus and learning to live your life as he would live it if he were you. Read that again, slowly. While much more could be said, this brief snapshot of the key coordinates of an existential map shaped by the Christian story will suffice going forward.

22. Willard, *Knowing Christ Today*, 51–53.

Let's turn now to our second condition concerning how to live a distinctively Christian philosophical way of life. Practitioners of this way of being in the world have their lives and everyday practices ordered by the Christian existential map as described above. This means that practitioners of a distinctively Christian philosophical way of life conduct their lives in such a way that they are *ready* to act, and indeed *do* reliably act, as if the above answers to *the reality question, the good-life question*, and *the character-formation question* are true and as if rival visions of reality and the good life are false; they *rely* on the "good deposit" as trustworthy and stable enough to build their lives on (Matt. 7:24–27).

To believe (and not simply *profess* to believe) that the truly good life is the one that is interactively engaged with the triune God and pervaded with love for God and others entails a readiness to act in such a way that the pursuit of money, unbridled pleasure, fame, or power over others is not the chief aim of your life. The moments of your day, the days of your week, the weeks of your month, the months of your year, and the years of your life are not defined by actions aimed at securing these ends above all else. These are not distinctively Christian ways of being in the world precisely *because* they are life-postures and pursuits that do not reflect the contours of the only true and satisfying existential map of reality and the good life, the Christian story. You may be living philosophically in some sense if you, say, view the pursuit of pleasure as the greatest good and order your life around the pursuit of pleasure, but you are most certainly not living a *Christian* philosophical way of life.

Finally, let's turn to our third condition for what it means to live a distinctively Christian philosophical way of life: the life and practices of practitioners of this way of life are grace-empowered, aimed at truth, and responsive to evidence.

As Hadot carefully points out in a chapter titled "Ancient Spiritual Exercises and 'Christian Philosophy,'" the very same spiritual exercises that were considered essential to philosophy as a way of life in antiquity—meditation, self-examination, attention, memorization, and others—were also part of a distinctively Christian philosophical way of life in antiquity.[23] Consider the following remark by the early church father Gregory of Nyssa (ca. 335–395) regarding the ingredients of a distinctively Christian philosophical way of life: "Now the details of the life of him who has chosen to live in such a *philosophy* as this [that is, in a Christian philosophical way of life], the things to be avoided, the *exercises* to be engaged in, the *rules* of temperance, the whole method of the *training*, and all the *daily regimen* which contributes towards this great end, has been dealt with in certain written manuals of instruction for the benefit of those who love details."[24] For Christians who desire to live philosophically, there is a vast world of wonders to be moved by, there are spiritual exercises to be practiced, and there is a tried-and-true method of grace-empowered soul training—a "daily regimen."[25]

So what exactly is the difference between the philosophical therapeutics or soul training (*askesis*) undertaken by Greek, Hellenistic, and Roman philosophers and those of Christian philosophers in

---

23. It is important to note, however, that Hadot does go on to lay the blame on select medieval Christian thinkers for the shift from philosophy as a way of life to philosophy as a merely intellectual enterprise that is subservient to theology as its handmaiden. As others have pointed out, Hadot's "decline narrative" runs the risk of oversimplifying things and needs to be highly qualified, if not rejected outright. See Sharpe and Ure, *Philosophy as a Way of Life*, 138–50; Bauerschmidt, *Thomas Aquinas*, 73–81.

24. "On Virginity," in *Gregory of Nyssa*, 368 (emphasis added).

25. It is interesting to note that in several places throughout his writings, the apostle Paul himself draws a close parallel between bodily training and training for godliness (1 Cor. 9:27; 1 Tim. 4:8), between bodily training and spiritual *askesis* in Christ. For further discussion of the idea that Christianity was understood as the "true philosophy" in antiquity, along with the idea that the Christian philosophical life included the notion of soul training, see the sources outlined in Hadot, *Philosophy as a Way of Life*, chap. 4.

antiquity? Hadot points out that Christian philosophers practiced the spiritual exercises in a distinctively Christian manner in that "they always presupposed the assistance of God's grace, and they made humility the most important of virtues."[26] For Christian philosophers in antiquity, the spiritual exercises that were thought to make practitioners fit to properly see and orient themselves to reality were *grace-empowered* and *grace-sustained*. Practitioners humbly relied on the necessary divine resources to bring about the needed transformation of the self.

A distinctively Christian philosophical way of life, then, is one that is marked by the humble recognition that genuine and lasting transformation in the power of the self (or flesh, *sarx*) is impossible; self-perfection and full freedom from "the passions of the flesh, which wage war against your soul" (1 Pet. 2:11), are hopeless given our ruined condition apart from divine grace. Only by being renewed in Christ by the work of his Spirit can the "deceitful desires" of the flesh be bridled (Eph. 4:22, see also Gal. 5:16; Rom. 7:13–25) and our minds be illuminated and restored to proper health (Eph. 4:18). Then no longer will we be alienated from the life of God, who is the highest good for which we were made. Non-Christian ancient philosophers knew nothing of the jaw-dropping wonder of grace.

The practitioner of a distinctively Christian philosophical way of life will engage in the regular practice of grace-empowered spiritual exercises that serve a threefold purpose as *channels*, *correctives*, and *preventatives*.[27] As *channels*, the spiritual exercises can serve as the regular means by which God's transformative grace flows into the soul of the practitioner, gradually shaping the practitioner into a certain kind of person—namely, one whose mind and heart are

---

26. Hadot, *Philosophy as a Way of Life*, 139.
27. I owe this insight about the corrective and preventative role of the spiritual exercises to Grimm and Cohoe, "What Is Philosophy as a Way of Life?"

purified in Christ and thus are more apt to see what truly is, to love and pursue the goods and ends that are most worth pursuing, and to order his or her everyday life accordingly.

As *correctives*, the spiritual exercises can help correct false visions of reality and the good life and dampen their allure. Just as regular physical training can help develop "muscle memory" that serves to reinforce proper movements of the body, so too regular soul training can develop "soul memory" that serves to reinforce proper movements of the soul. For example, when I am lured away by a false vision of the good life—say, that the satisfaction of illicit desire is the highest good worthy of pursuit—the embodied ("in the bones") knowledge I have acquired by way of the spiritual exercises (fasting, solitude, self-examination) concerning "the passions of the flesh, which wage war against your soul" (1 Pet. 2:11), helps correct my perceived need to reach out and satisfy my illicit desire.

Finally, as *preventatives*, the embodied knowledge created by the spiritual exercises can help hinder false visions of reality and of the good life from arising in the first place. If God, by his grace, has enlisted the spiritual exercises for the purpose of "training us to renounce ungodliness and worldly passions, and to live self-controlled, upright, and godly lives" (Titus 2:11–12), then we can draw the needed spiritual strength and health from them to stand firm in this way. And just as a healthy body can act as a preventative for future physical ailments, so too a healthy soul that has been formed by way of the exercises can act as a preventative for future spiritual ailments. In sum, regular, Spirit-empowered soul training, or *askesis*, can help rightly order our heads, hearts, and hands and keep them attuned to what is genuinely true, good, and beautiful in Christ. Such training enables us to live *wisely* in the biblical sense of the word.

Throughout the next two chapters, I'll set out to illustrate what the Christian philosophical life looks like "on the ground," so to speak. I'll first play the role of philosophical physician and diagnose two existential ailments of our modern condition that hinder our ability to clearly see and align ourselves to the natural grain of reality (chap. 5). Then, in chapter 6, I'll show how the Christian philosophical life can serve as a therapeutic remedy—as Lady Philosophy would put it—for these two life-threatening ailments and how it can help us orient ourselves and hold fast to what is true, good, and beautiful in Christ.

5

Diagnosing Our
Existential Ailments

Thus far we have seen what it means to live philosophically as a
Christian and I have spotlighted a particular historical example from
Boethius's *Consolation of Philosophy* of how Christian philosophy
as a way of life can be medicinal or therapeutic for its practitioners.
Recall the gentler and stronger remedies of Lady Philosophy that
helped cure the prisoner of his sickly existential state and bring about
a clearer vision of reality and a greater health of soul. Philosophy is,
as one early church father put it, "that medicine of the soul . . . from
which we learn the remedy for every weakness that can touch the
soul."[1] In this chapter I'll aim to diagnose two modern existential ailments, and in the next chapter I'll show how living philosophically as
a Christian can serve as a potent, life-giving remedy for each ailment.

1. "On Virginity," in *Gregory of Nyssa*, 368.

Ailment No. 1: Our Metaphysical and Moral Vertigo

The Promethean Ideal

According to German sociologist Hartmut Rosa, the now settled posture of the contemporary mind is the obsessive tendency to control and master the world, to expand humanity's share of the world and make it useful for our desired purposes, to be—in Descartes's words—"masters and possessors of nature."[2] This deeply settled, modern posture carries with it a view about how we ought to see and relate to the world at large: everything else exists for the sake of our own individual and collective desires and can and should be mastered accordingly.

This modern posture of mastery and human control has a markedly different feel to it than our instinctive human impulse to improve our lives through interacting with and managing the world as we find it. Rather, in its extreme modern expression, this stance has morphed into an all-pervasive *way of being* in the world, an existential posture that aims to bring *all* things given in creation before the realm of human will and desire.

At its worst, this distinctively modern way of being in the world can take the form of "playing God." Philosopher David McPherson refers to this way of being in the world as "the Promethean ideal," alluding to the Greek tragedy featuring Prometheus, a titan who stole godlike power (fire) from the Olympian gods and gave it to humans so they could acquire greater technical mastery over the world.[3]

---

2. Descartes, *Discourse on Method*, 35; see also Rosa, *Uncontrollability of the World*. For a similar diagnosis of our modern condition and its tendency to instrumentalize everything under the sun, see Taylor, *Malaise of Modernity*, chap. 9.

3. In what follows, I draw heavily from McPherson, *Virtues of Limits*, chap. 1. Compare Gen. 1:28 and Gen. 2:15 with Gen. 11:1–9 for healthy and unhealthy examples of this posture.

The Promethean ideal, which manifests itself in a deep drive to wield godlike power and obtain mastery over the world, now extends to every aspect of human life, from the beginning of life to its end and every stage in between.[4] We now strive to tailor the genetic features of our children in accordance with our desired preferences (genetic engineering and so-called designer babies) and to control both the timing and the terms of our own deaths (physician-assisted suicide and so-called right to die). Silicon Valley is filled with wealthy visionaries and entrepreneurs who are, at present, investing mind-bending amounts of money into companies whose stated aim is to "solve death" by examining it as a "technical glitch" that awaits a "technical solution."[5]

Moreover, the Promethean ideal as a deep-seated way of life may also explain why we are now seeing the novel attempt to bring certain domains of human life, domains that were previously *received* and understood as *given*, under the control of the human will. Here I am thinking about certain philosophical ideologies that view aspects of reality such as race, biological age, gender/sex, and even human nature itself as *plastic* and *manipulable*, capable of being shaped by our will and desires.[6]

But, as Rosa insightfully points out, there is a paradox at the heart of the Promethean ideal as a distinctively modern way of being in the world: The more we strive to master reality and shape it according to our own will and purposes, the more we lose our grip on reality and become increasingly detached from it. The more we try to bend and shape what belongs to the natural grain of reality regarding God,

4. Rosa details the pervasiveness of this posture throughout all human life in chap. 6 of his book *The Uncontrollability of the World*.
5. Harari, *Homo Deus*, 23.
6. For an intellectual history of how we got to where we are on this score, see Trueman, *Rise and Triumph of the Modern Self*; or (shorter) Trueman, *Strange New World*.

ourselves, and the world around us, the more alienated we become from God, ourselves, and the world around us.

Unsurprisingly, the Promethean ideal gives rise to a kind of existential vertigo or disorientation, an inability to clearly see and hold fast to a stable point of reference regarding the real and the good, including who we are and what our proper place is in the grand scheme of things. This existential vertigo that comes in the wake of the Promethean ideal can be both *metaphysical* (e.g., concerning our relation to reality, human nature and identity, and so on) and *moral* (e.g., concerning our understanding and pursuit of the good life and what kind of life is ultimately worth living), and it can affect both Christian and non-Christian alike.

Acedia as Spiritual and Moral Lethargy

Life-threatening moral vertigo can come in many shapes and sizes and can afflict Christian and non-Christian alike. Indeed, there is a kind of moral vertigo that involves the failure to be properly responsive to what is truly good and fulfilling in human life. It is possible to become so existentially disoriented that we—whether Christian or non-Christian—become morally and spiritually calloused, no longer moved by what is spiritually and morally weighty and worthy of our moral care and action.

Much older and wiser Christians used to call this grave spiritual ailment *acedia* (from the Greek word *akedia*, meaning "lack of care"). In the Christian tradition, acedia, often called *sloth*, is itself a complex and multifaceted moral vice.[7] As an inner condition of the soul, the root of acedia turns out to be a disregard for or an

---

7. For a helpful place to begin exploring this vice in more detail, see DeYoung, *Glittering Vices*, chap. 5. In fact, as the ancients pointed out, acedia has many "daughters"—other moral vices that are produced by acedia—including pride. See Thomas Aquinas, *Summa theologiae* II-II, q. 35, art. 4, ad. 2.

active resistance to one's wholehearted commitment to and love for God. As creatures made to thrive in loving friendship with God—our greatest and highest good—human beings were made to receive and to cultivate a greater love for God (Matt. 22:36–40). As friendship with God deepens, God's love increasingly transforms us, putting to death our wayward loves and restructuring our inner lives to be in conformity with that of Jesus Christ. This is, at bottom, our primary identity and vocation as human beings. Acedia actively hinders us from fulfilling the very purpose of our existence, the cultivation of a greater love for God and others. And this is precisely why the Christian tradition has understood acedia to be one of the deadliest spiritual ailments under the sun.

Ailment No. 2: Our Ailing Sight and Attention

Visual Overload

As of the year 2023, researchers are on the verge of mind-boggling medical innovations that have the potential to render physical blindness a thing of the past. With the advent of technologies such as bionic eyes (check out Phoenix99 or Pixium Vision on the internet) and novel gene therapies (see Luxturna), many believe that we are entering the frontier of a new and improved way of seeing the world that is available to anyone, or at least available to those who can pay for it.

But what if, in the midst of these medical marvels that increase our capacity for *physical* sight, we are steadily losing our ability to *truly* see the world? Consider these timely and insightful words from German Christian philosopher Josef Pieper (1904–1997): "Man's ability to *see* is in decline. Those who nowadays concern themselves with culture and education will experience this fact again and again. We do not mean here, of course, the physiological sensitivity of the human eye. We mean the spiritual capacity to perceive the visible reality as it truly is."[8] It's an interesting thought, isn't it—losing our ability to see *in the midst of* flashy new medical technologies? But for those who know and trust the scriptural witness, this idea of seeing but not *truly* seeing and of hearing but not *truly* hearing should be very familiar (Deut. 29:4; Isa. 6:9; Jer. 5:21; Matt. 13:13–17). While our sensory faculty of sight might be working properly (even better than ever!), we may fail to be attuned to reality as it actually *is* rather than as we prefer it to be.

But why should this steady decline in our ability to see and attend to truth, beauty, and goodness bother us? Here's what I tell my students: our ability to *care* for things as they are is directly related to our ability to *see* and *attend* to them as they are. If a doctor lacks the ability to discern and carefully attend to the human body as it actually is, she will not be able to properly identify a particular illness that afflicts the body. And if she cannot properly identify the bodily illness, she will not be able to properly diagnose the patient and prescribe the best course of treatment. Her inability to see and attend to reality as it is directly hinders her ability to properly care for the patient. In the same way, if I'm suffering from existential dullness of sight—a diminished ability to truly see the world as it is—I will be unable to properly identify what is truly real, good, and beautiful in human life. As a result, I will be unable to live along the grain of reality, let alone help you do the same. In the words of Jesus, "If the blind lead the blind, both will fall into a pit" (Matt. 15:14).

I think Pieper is spot on in his diagnosis: we are steadily losing our ability to see and carefully attend to what is genuinely good, true, and beautiful in human life. What's even more interesting is one of the reasons Pieper gives for *why* he thinks we're losing this ability.

8. Pieper, *Only the Lover Sings*, 31.

According to Pieper, "The average person of our time loses the ability to see because *there is too much to see!*"[9] Paradoxical, isn't it? Most of us are no doubt familiar with the idea that too much audible noise can make it more difficult to hear or attend to what demands our focused attention. If you are a parent, you know this reality well. When you are in a noisy environment, so noisy that you are unable to attend to the cries of your children, it's a rather discomforting feeling. In the same way, Pieper thinks that a flood of "visual noise . . . makes clear perception impossible."[10]

It will be worthwhile to further explore the idea that the saturation of "visual noise" in our lives steadily diminishes our ability to truly see the world: when things get visually noisier, we run the risk of losing sight of truth itself, the truth about reality within (ourselves) and reality without (the world).

Let's start with the reality within: we are steadily losing our ability to be aware of the shape and texture of our own souls, in large part because of the visually noisy and fast-paced rhythms that shape our lives. We are so busy gazing outward at all there is to see and take in that we never really stop to gaze inward and examine who we truly are and who we are becoming. If the visual noise and lightning pace of our lives squeeze out any time and space for self-examination, we will gradually lose the once-cherished prize of self-knowledge, the ability to accurately know ourselves and our proper place in relation to God and others.[11]

There is a real danger in our failing to properly know ourselves, one that is woefully neglected among Christians and non-Christians alike. One particularly deadly consequence of our inability to truly know ourselves is that we can fall into the snare of self-deception. The

9. Pieper, *Only the Lover Sings*, 32.
10. Pieper, *Only the Lover Sings*, 33.
11. Calvin, *Institutes of the Christian Religion*, 35.

apostle John reminds us of the very real possibility of self-deception when he says, "If we say we have no sin, we deceive ourselves, and the truth is not in us" (1 John 1:8). Imagine being so completely out of touch with yourself that you sincerely think that you are without sin, that you've morally and spiritually "arrived," so to speak. With moral clarity and insight, the apostle John tells us that when we are self-deceived about who we really are and the moral shape of our life, *the truth is not in us*. When our ability to see ourselves is clouded, we thereby lose a healthy connection to the truth about ourselves that is essential for us to live well in relation to God and others.

In fact, those who are self-deceived more often than not manage their beliefs with little regard for the truth—the very definition of "self-deception," according to Jean-Paul Sartre.[12] The self-deceived are prone to believe what they believe—about politics, sexual ethics, religion, entertainment, success, relationships, and so forth—because it is useful or socially acceptable, or because it is what people of their tribe are *supposed* to believe. Consequently, truth takes a back seat to managing one's appearance, power, and social status.

An overload of visual noise causes us to lose sight of the reality outside us as well. As every square inch of our lives becomes increasingly bombarded with visual noise—from the moment we awake to the moment we go to sleep—we are in danger of gradually losing sight of truth itself. And this is exactly why this loss of existential sight is so life-threatening. If we lose the ability to see who we truly are and what ends are ultimately worth pursuing in human life, we thereby lose the ability to successfully order our lives along the grain of reality (and thus we also forfeit the ability to live *wisely*, in a biblical sense).

There is no question that our current cultural environment in the West is awash in a bottomless sea of information and data. We've

---

12. This observation from Sartre on self-deception is drawn from Ten Elshof, *I Told Me So*, 27.

become gradually accustomed to the constant waves of information and digital stimuli that flood our every waking moment, overwhelming us with an ever-increasing amount of visual noise. As G. K. Chesterton once put it, "People are inundated, blinded, deafened, and mentally paralyzed by a flood of vulgar and tasteless externals, leaving them no time for leisure, thought, or creation from within themselves."[13]

The alarming fact is that an increasing amount of the information we take in each day from the news, social media, and the internet is deliberately misleading in some way or other. Information that misleads us—whether by deliberately communicating a falsehood or by spinning some bit of truth, either by presenting only a part of the story (cherry-picking) or by presenting the whole story but doing so in a biased or unfair manner—is what we now commonly refer to as "fake news." While fake news itself is not a unique phenomenon of our digital age, electronic media has made the spread of misleading information much easier and has increased the financial incentive for spreading it. There are now extremely powerful financial incentives motivating people to get you to read or listen to misleading information about religion, politics, economics, world affairs, the environment, and so forth. Information that distorts a clear-eyed vision of reality has now become big business.

In his excellent book *Beyond Fake News*, Christian philosopher Justin McBrayer provides a very helpful picture for thinking about our current information environment—our "information-scape"—along the lines of a physical landscape.[14] Just as a physical landscape can be filled with beauty that is eclipsed by thick pollution and widespread litter, so too our information-scape can be replete with

---

13. Chesterton reportedly made this comment during a lecture given at the University of Toronto in 1930 titled "Culture and the Coming Peril." Quoted in Caldecott, *Beauty for Truth's Sake*, 20.
14. McBrayer, *Beyond Fake News*, 3.

"informational litter" that distorts our ability to truly see the world and to lay hold of truth. And the question is not *whether* we inhabit an information-scape but, rather, *which* one we inhabit and just *how* polluted it is. And, just as a polluted physical landscape can have a severe impact on one's health, so too a polluted information-scape can have a severe impact on the clarity and health of one's mind and heart.[15]

So how do we see our way through the informational litter that so easily distorts our vision of the truth? The frightening reality is that the very filters many of us use to sift through the landfill of misinformation—digital technologies and media platforms (internet, social media, etc.)—themselves influence "which content you see and how you navigate that swollen environment."[16] In other words, the very tools that many of us depend on to navigate our information-scape actively *contribute* to our increasingly distorted vision of reality.

Let me briefly explain. It is no secret that tech giants such as Google, Twitter, and Meta use algorithms to strategically place targeted stories and advertisements in your information feed. In his book, McBrayer explains (and documents) this reality in detail:

> These algorithms are designed to manipulate you into acting in some way, for example, buy something or to click on a link. Using your personal details and your past history, sites like Facebook can predict which news stories you will share, which products you are likely to purchase, and so forth. It then uses this information to sort the millions of available articles and stories to just a handful that you'll see. The articles and stories most likely to get you to act are the ones that got people *just like you* to act. The result is a carefully crafted news bubble in which your Facebook feed and Twitter networks expose you

---

15. Another outstanding book devoted to this topic is Bilbro, *Reading the Times*.
16. McBrayer, *Beyond Fake News*, 15.

to controversial views you antecedently accept and exclude contrary viewpoints.[17]

It turns out, then, that the way in which most of us receive and filter information today is greatly influenced by our own ideological opinions and biases. We are left, then, with an information network—an "epistemic bubble"—that is *made in our own image*, one that looks a lot like us and tends to exclude religious, political, and moral viewpoints that are different from our own. And when we live in an epistemic bubble long enough, we will inevitably find ourselves in an "echo chamber" where we come to perceive ideological outsiders not only as mistaken but as deceptive, malicious, and manipulative. In an echo chamber, dissenters are perceived not only as wrong but also as people who can't be trusted.[18]

But epistemic bubbles and echo chambers are extremely risky epistemic environments because they tend to distort our perception of the truth as well as our perception of the intrinsic value of other divine image bearers. When we become trapped in an epistemic bubble or echo chamber, we lose sight of our own intellectual limitations and fallibility (we could be wrong, after all), and we forfeit precious opportunities to be corrected and guided back to the truth when our own views fail to match the way things are.

A Crisis of Attention

As ever-increasing amounts of visual noise become our new normal, we will continue to be afflicted with what one author calls the "crisis of attention."[19] There are at any given moment a countless

---

17. McBrayer, *Beyond Fake News*, 16.
18. I owe the terms "epistemic bubble" and "echo chamber" to Nguyen, "Escape the Echo Chamber."
19. Crawford, *World beyond Your Head*, 1–27.

number of competing spectacles vying for your attention—for your eyes, your ears, and ultimately your heart (Matt. 6:21). Just as information and personal data have become units of economic exchange in the information economy, so too our attention has become a unit of economic exchange in what some have called the "attention economy."[20] People are making money, lots and lots of money, off your attention. Major corporations are keenly aware of the economic benefit of capturing your attention, even for a moment, which is why tech giant Meta made just shy of $115,000,000,000 (that's 115 *billion* dollars) in ad revenues alone in 2021.[21] Our attention has now become monetized in a way that is unprecedented in human history, and many of us are more than happy to give it away for free.

Yet our attention isn't just of economic and financial interest but is an essential feature of the moral life in general. What we attend to minute by minute, hour by hour, day by day will *inevitably* shape us; we eventually come to resemble what we behold. This is why the Bible, with striking clarity and moral insight, places such a strong emphasis on the moral importance of attending to and imitating those who virtuously embody the truth, goodness, and beauty of the Christian life.[22]

And, given the very real dynamics of human sin this side of Eden, we all struggle against a powerful, inherited tendency to fix our attention on all the wrong things (or, at least, not on the weightiest things). As the apostle John pointed out long ago, these "desires of the eyes" are "not from the Father but . . . from the world" (1 John 2:16). It

---

20. See Odell, *How to Do Nothing*; Crawford, *World beyond Your Head*.

21. Meta Investor Relations, "Meta Reports Fourth Quarter and Full Year 2021 Results," news release, February 2, 2022, https://investor.fb.com/investor-news/press-release-details/2022/Meta-Reports-Fourth-Quarter-and-Full-Year-2021-Results/default.aspx.

22. See 1 Cor. 4:16; 11:1; Eph. 5:1; 1 Thess. 1:6; 2:14; 2 Thess. 3:7, 9; Heb. 6:12; 13:7; 3 John 11.

turns out that our eyes tend to hunger for all the wrong things: they inordinately desire or lust after things that are in direct conflict with God's morally weighty and meaningful purposes for us and others. One author defines *spectacle* as "something that captures human attention, an instant when our eyes and brains focus and fixate on something projected at us."[23] *Empty* and *vain* spectacle, then, involves our attention being captivated by something that lacks moral substance, is trivial, or is outright morally disordered. If I focus on climbing over my coworkers for that next promotion, seeing others solely as means of entertainment and amusement,[24] or if I focus on making sure that I'm seen by others as belonging to the "right" social group, standing for the "right" social causes, driving the "right" kind of car, holding the "right" political and social positions, and so forth, I fall prey to the lure of empty and vain spectacle. Consequently, our wayward eyes need to be trained and formed to attend to matters of moral and spiritual gravity. We are in dire need of an *askesis* of our attention.[25]

23. Reinke, *Competing Spectacles*, 14.
24. Postman, *Amusing Ourselves to Death*.
25. Crawford, *World beyond Your Head*, 15.

6

Christian Philosophical Remedies for Our Existential Ailments

We've peered at the medical chart of our modern age, and the diagnosis doesn't look promising. We've seen that our moral and metaphysical vertigo and our ailing loss of sight and attention undermine our ability to see reality and thus live wisely along its natural grain. I now want to employ the medical model of Christian philosophizing to explore how living philosophically as a Christian can serve as a potent and health-giving remedy for our modern existential ailments. In doing so, my aim is to illustrate what a Christian philosophical way of life looks like "on the ground." We can put it this way: If Lady Philosophy were to grace us with a visit today and take note of our existential ailments, what might her gentler and stronger remedies be for *our* sickly soul condition? And, believe it or not, our own existential ailments are not all that novel.

Let's start by restating the three conditions at the heart of a Christian philosophical way of life (CPWL), which were outlined in chapter 4:

1. *Commit to an existential map shaped by the Christian story*: Practitioners of a CPWL are committed to "the faith that was once for all delivered to the saints" (Jude 3) as the existential map that specifies what truly *is* and what *ought to be*.

2. *Orient your life around a Christian existential map*: Practitioners of a CPWL have their life and practices oriented around the vision of reality and the good life shaped by the Christian story.

3. *Engage in grace-empowered, truth-directed practices*: The life and everyday practices of practitioners of a CPWL are grace-empowered, aimed at truth, and responsive to evidence.

Let's look at each of these in turn as it relates to our two existential maladies.

Let's start with condition 1. When we commit to an existential map shaped by the Christian story, we thereby commit to a host of coordinates that we believe rightly reflect what is real, true, and morally good. In regard to *the reality question* (what is real?), we (re)commit ourselves first and foremost to a vision of reality that treasures the triune God as supreme over all, who is the origin and fount of all created reality, and in his wisdom (Prov. 8:22–36) has constructed a natural grain to reality that is truly good and beautiful; indeed, this natural grain to reality evokes delight in the heart of God (Prov. 8:30–31). While humans may try to suppress, twist, and distort creation's natural moral grain (Rom. 1:19–32)—including what it means to be human (what human beings *are*) and what constitutes the truly happy and flourishing human life (what human beings are *for*)—this natural grain is not subject to human will or desire; it cannot itself be altered by cultural pressure or by the next presidential election.

In regard to *the good-life question* and *the character-formation question*, and in sharp contrast to the Promethean ideal, we flourish morally when we humbly receive and stand in wonder of God's creational ideal and don't try to revolt against it or bend it to fit our own desires. And those who discern and lovingly receive this "good way" and continue to "walk in it" will find rest for their souls (Jer. 6:16; Matt. 11:28–30); those who fail to discern it or who shake their fist at it injure themselves (Prov. 8:36).

When it comes to our loss of sight and attention, we (re)commit ourselves to the revealed reality that we were divinely made to see and lay hold of the truth—ultimately, God as the supreme Truth. We were created with a deep metaphysical hunger for wonder and for truth that can be satisfied only by turning away from distorted visions of reality and of the good life and by fitting our lives into God's creational pattern, the way of wisdom. According to the Christian story, our primary human vocation is to "taste and see that the LORD is good" (Ps. 34:8) and to seek after the "one thing" for which we were made, to "dwell in the house of the LORD" and "to gaze upon the beauty of the LORD" (Ps. 27:4). We were created to experience soul-satisfying wonder in the face of the triune God, whether imperfectly here and now or perfectly in the vision of God in the life to come. And, just as Lady Philosophy had to administer potent doses of truth to remind the sickly prisoner of what is truly real and truly good, so too do we need regular potent doses of truth to remind us of what is true and good according to the Christian existential map and its many coordinates.

Let's turn now to condition 2, regarding how the Christian philosophical life might serve as a therapeutic for our modern existential ailments. As I previously noted in chapter 4, living philosophically as a Christian involves more than just mentally assenting to a Christian existential map of reality and the good life. If we are living a distinctively *Christian* philosophical way of life, the steady rhythms of our lives—*who* we are and what we *do* (what we devote our time, resources, energies to)—will be informed by and anchored in a Christian vision of reality and the good life.

But what might a way of life that is intentionally anchored in and ordered by the metaphysical and moral coordinates of the Christian story look like "on the ground"? More importantly, what might such a life look like in contrast to the ways of life on display in the Promethean ideal and evidenced by our ailing sight and attention?

A Christian philosophical way of life will undoubtedly be marked by steady rhythms of life that are on a crash course with the Promethean ideal. One of the most important counter-rhythms, anchored in and ordered by a Christian existential map, is the steady acknowledgment and embrace of our God-given, existential limitations. We are not God, nor could we ever possibly know better than God how best to order our lives; rather, we are existentially fragile and dependent and draw our fullness of life and moment-by-moment existence from God, the architect and end of our creaturely nature (Rom. 11:36). We are not infinitely resourceful and self-sufficient as a species; rather, "man shall not live by bread alone, but by every word that comes from the mouth of God" (Matt. 4:4; see also Deut. 8:3). We are not "masters and possessors of nature," and the true remedy for our ruined condition is not found in scientific and technological advancement, our modern equivalent of the "chariots" and "horsemen" that can so easily become the idolatrous grounds of our ultimate hope (Isa. 31:1). Rather, we are made to be wise stewards of God's creational design, to "look to the Holy One of Israel" (Isa. 31:1) and humbly walk in his "ancient paths" and find rest for our souls (Jer. 6:16). In sharp contrast to the Promethean ideal, then, we should not aim to try to shake free of or shake our fist at our God-given creaturely limitations; indeed, doing so would be futile and would inevitably lead to living against the grain of reality. Our limits, dependence, and deep need for God for our lasting fulfillment are built-in features—even gifts—of human existence, not bugs.[1]

Let me try to be even more specific. When it comes to how I treat my physical body throughout my day, I humbly receive the fact that I am, by nature and design, a bodily creature who runs on finite physical resources and needs regular sleep, nourishment, rest, and physical care. I receive and respect these bodily limits; I don't fight against them and try to live well despite them. I also embrace the God-ordained reality that I am not my own and that my "body is not meant for sexual immorality, but for the Lord" (1 Cor. 6:13). This means that I live *against* the natural grain of reality if I assume a posture of bodily and sexual autonomy and mastery, treating my body and my sexuality as fluid and capable of being put to whatever purposes I see fit. When it comes to my sexuality, I honor my body, and thereby glorify God *in* my body, by living in accordance with the inherent, God-given ends for which the body was made. By contrast, when I live against these ends, I dishonor my body and fail to glorify God in my body (Rom. 1:24–27). Indeed, I even run the risk of self-injury (Prov. 8:36) insofar as I sin against my own body (1 Cor. 6:18).

Over and against the Promethean way of being in the world, the Christian philosophical way of life will be marked by the cultivation of what philosopher David McPherson calls "limiting virtues," such as humility, reverence (expressing awe and respect for what is truly worthy of awe and respect), contentment, gratitude, and loyalty to God's moral design for our flourishing. The limiting virtues are stable character traits that enable us to be properly responsive to what is genuinely good, sacred, worthy of wonder and reverence *for its own sake*. These weighty moral goods rightly make demands on what we *should* will and desire in the first place.

---

1. For an excellent book-length treatment of the idea that we were created with a deep existential and relational need for God, see McKirland, *God's Provision*.

The limiting virtue of humility in particular "ensures that we recognize and live out our proper place in the scheme of things, and it is
concerned, among other things, with reining in the tendency to 'play
God.'"[2] The limiting virtues help us to be alive and humbly attentive
to all that is truly wonderful and weighty in human life: the real, the
good, and the beautiful. They awaken us out of our spiritual and
moral lethargy (*acedia*) and make us more responsive to—rather than
masters and possessors of—God's morally significant and satisfying
purposes for creation, all so that we can better see and "take hold of
that which is truly life" (1 Tim. 6:19).

What I'm saying here is that the limiting virtues—humility in
particular—act as potent, life-giving remedies for our modern moral
and existential vertigo. A way of life defined by the limiting virtues
serves as a proper corrective to both the Promethean ideal and acedia
in that such a life "is concerned with giving proper recognition to
self-transcending sources of value that place constraints on our will
and thereby help to define our proper place in the scheme of things."[3]

How might a Christian philosophical way of life serve as a remedy
to our increasing dullness of sight and attention? A Christian philosophical way of life will be marked by life-patterns and rhythms that
are aimed both at clearing away the excess visual noise that distorts a
clear-eyed vision of the real and the good—including the visual noise
of misinformation and the lure of empty and vain spectacle—and at
positively cultivating our God-given capacity to truly see the world
and be properly responsive to it.

Clearing away excess visual noise and learning to truly see the
world and become more responsive to it will inevitably involve cultivating certain virtuous habits of mind philosophers call *intellectual
virtues*. Intellectually virtuous people—those who have cultivated a

2. McPherson, *Virtues of Limits*, 28–29.
3. McPherson, *Virtues of Limits*, 30.

virtuous intellectual character—carefully attend to their own beliefs, the reasons that support those beliefs, and the process by which those beliefs were formed (*intellectual care* and *attentiveness*); they strive to be aware of, own, and correct for their intellectual limitations and blind spots (*intellectual humility*); they avoid playing fast and loose with the truth for the sake of personal gain (*intellectual honesty*); they "transcend their own perspectives by taking the merits of other views seriously" (*intellectual open-mindedness*); they "think as well of others' intelligence and intellectual character as they reasonably can" (*intellectual charity*); they "hold on to their well-supported beliefs unless given good reasons for revising them"[4] (*intellectual firmness*); and they continue to uphold their well-supported beliefs in the face of great risk and loss, such as loss of social status (*intellectual courage*).

These virtuous habits of mind are cultivated over a long period of time and, once acquired, become like deep grooves that guide the way we act and navigate the world—in this case, how responsive we are to truth and the reasons for and against our beliefs. They gradually form and shape us into the *kinds of people* who are more likely than not to truly see and lay hold of God's creational ideal, for the sake of living wisely.

Those who increasingly put on intellectually virtuous character will navigate the information and attention economies in a different manner. They will actively seek to become more aware of how their own information-scape is littered with misinformation at every turn and how they might do their part to clean it up and to help others do the same. Because they value wisdom for living and aim to cultivate a virtuous intellectual character, they will take steps to carefully monitor the sources and content of their information intake and will not be reckless with the truth for the sake of personal gain, power, or winning points with their peers or with their wider ideological tribe.

4. King, *Excellent Mind*, 254.

They will aim, as best they can, to be on the lookout for their own echo chambers and epistemic bubbles and will strive to escape them and pop them when they can, and they will patiently try to help others do the same. They will recognize that they inhabit a bustling information and attention economy, one in which there are countless empty and vain spectacles that compete for their attention and, ultimately, for their heart and their mind. They will recognize and strive to resist the very real temptation to confuse mere *information acquisition* with the cultivation of genuine *wisdom* for living well.

Spiritual Exercises, Soul *Askesis*, and the Christian Philosophical Way of Life

Finally, let's turn to condition 3, which involves engaging in spiritual exercises that are grace-empowered, aimed at truth, and responsive to evidence. What are the various kinds of spiritual exercises that can serve as potent remedies for our two modern existential ailments?

We've already seen in chapter 2 how and why the spiritual exercises should be viewed as one of the essential ingredients to a distinctively Christian philosophical way of life. To recap, the Christian spiritual exercises serve the following threefold purpose: they serve as *channels* of God's free and transformative grace that enable us to be receptive to what truly is and ought to be, as *correctives* that help chasten false visions of reality and the good life, and as *preventatives* to help keep false visions of realty and the good life from arising in the first place. Thus, grace-empowered spiritual practices form us into the *kinds of people* who reliably see, who are receptive to, and who steadily uphold what is genuinely true and good, and they enable us to live well and wisely along the grain of reality.

Historically, there are two general types of spiritual exercises that we find in the Christian tradition: what Dallas Willard calls *exercises of abstinence* and *exercises of engagement*.[5] Both types of spiritual exercises are rooted in the biblical mandate to actively cultivate our new life in Christ as well as to uproot the sinful and twisted patterns of seeing, feeling, and behaving that once characterized our old life in Adam (Col. 3:1–10). As indicated in Romans 13:14, the driving purpose of these two different types of soul-training exercises is to "put on the Lord Jesus Christ, and make no provision for the flesh, to gratify its desires."

Some spiritual practices—*exercises of engagement*—train us to *put on* the Christlike ways of seeing, feeling, and behaving by the enabling power of the Holy Spirit. Other spiritual practices—*exercises of abstinence*—train us to *put off* (better: *kill* or *put to death*; see Col. 3:5) the worldly ways of seeing, feeling, and behaving that are no longer fitting for those who are in Christ. Peter says, "As sojourners and exiles . . . *abstain* from the passions of the flesh, which wage war against your soul" (1 Pet. 2:11).

Solitude and Silence

Let's start with some exercises of abstinence that provide potent remedies for our two modern existential ailments, the Promethean ideal and our failing sight and attention.

The spiritual exercises of *solitude* and *silence* are vital to the Christian philosophical life today. We can understand the exercises of solitude and silence as the practices of purposefully abstaining from social interaction and communication with others for the sake of realigning our wayward hearts and minds to God and his kingdom purposes in the world. Regular times of withdrawal to a place

---

5. Willard, *Spirit of the Disciplines*. For a shorter treatment of the role of the spiritual exercises in Christian formation, see Willard's essay "Living a Transformed Life," in Willard, *Renewing the Christian Mind*, 11–53.

of solitude and silence help us, as they helped Christ himself (Matt. 4:1–11; Mark 1:35–39; 6:30–32; Luke 5:15–16), to clear away the clutter of the soul and create space for a greater openness and responsiveness to God and the wonder of his life-giving presence. Solitude and silence rid us of our humanly crafted "scaffoldings": the people, positions, and social environments in which we try to find life apart from Christ and that tend to obstruct a clear-eyed vision of reality and of the life ultimately worth living.[6] No visual noise or glowing screens to divert our attention, no positions of power or honor to prop us up, no achievements to hide behind, no people to please or placate, nothing to turn to that will satisfy our soul's deep hunger other than God himself.

According to theologian and writer Henri Nouwen, solitude is "the furnace of transformation. Without solitude we remain victims of our society and continue to be entangled in the illusions of the false self."[7] The furnace of solitude and silence is where we go to be purged of our deep-seated tendency to find our core identity and value in comparing ourselves to others. Solitude and silence help us to identify and untangle ourselves from the shallow and ultimately fleeting pursuits that occupy our waking attention (2 Tim. 2:4) and to "lay aside every weight, and sin which clings so closely" (Heb. 12:1). Consequently, these two exercises help correct our distorted loves and patterns of social interaction and help us guard against sacrificing a clear vision of the truth (both about ourselves and about the world around us) on the altar of social approval and trying to find fullness of life in relation to others.

And, paradoxically, it is only by being purged of our relentless need to be "people-pleasers" (Col. 3:22) that we can truly be *for* others and will their good in Christ. For "in order to be of service to

---

6. See Nouwen, *Way of the Heart*, 27.
7. Nouwen, *Way of the Heart*, 25.

others we have to die to them; that is, we have to give up measuring our meaning and value with the yardstick of others."[8] Ironically, it is only by regularly withdrawing from others in due measure that we can truly move *closer* to them and be who we need to be *for* them.[9]

Self-Examination and Meditation

The exercises of *self-examination* and *meditation*, which often go hand in hand with solitude and silence, are two other vital soul-training exercises for Christians who aim to live philosophically in our current cultural moment. The exercise of self-examination is the practice of inviting God's loving presence to search and sift our minds and hearts and to lead us in the way of flourishing in Christ (Ps. 139:23–24; 1 Cor. 11:28; Phil. 1:9–10; Col. 1:9). The practice of self-examination has been a pillar of Christian formation down through the ages and is a deeply biblical practice (it is even required before one takes the Lord's Supper: 1 Cor. 11:28).[10] Through self-examination, we become increasingly aware of the many "hidden faults" (Ps. 19:12) that cloud our clear-eyed vision of reality and hinder our ability to live well along the grain of reality for God's glory and our good.

When we open ourselves to God in honesty and in truth in the light of his gracious presence (Ps. 139:23–24), we are led into greater depths of self-knowledge. Regularly opening the windows of the soul through self-examination allows the light of God to flood in and transform the hidden places of the heart. As a result, our ailing sight is gradually restored to behold "the light of the knowledge of

---

8. Nouwen, *Way of the Heart*, 35.
9. Nouwen, *Way of the Heart*, 39.
10. See Ignatius, *Spiritual Exercises*. Spiritual exercises 32–43 all pertain to the examination of conscience.

the glory of God in the face of Jesus Christ" (2 Cor. 4:6), who is himself the fount of the wisdom and knowledge we need to truly live well (Col. 2:3).

The exercise of *meditation* primarily involves the practice of cultivating a greater awareness of God's presence through prayerfully attending to his written Word through the guidance of the Holy Spirit (Josh. 1:8; Pss. 19:14; 119:15, 23, 48). From a biblical perspective, the purpose of meditation is, as contemplative spiritual writer Joyce Huggett puts it, "to see ourselves in the light of God's revealed word."[11] The truth is that we quite often fail to see ourselves and the world around us in the proper light. And it is only in the purifying and radiant light of God and his revealed truth that we truly see reality for what it is: "For with you is the fountain of life; in your light do we see light" (Ps. 36:9).

From the temptation narrative in Matthew 4:1–11 we learn that Jesus was able to clearly see and successfully resist the allure of false visions of reality and the good life *because of* his regular practice of meditation on Scripture and basking in the light of God's revealed truth about human nature (see v. 4) and about how only God is ultimately worthy of reverence and worship (see vv. 7, 10).

Though meditation is primarily concerned with fostering a greater awareness of God and his ways as revealed in Scripture, there is a wider sense of meditation that involves fixing our minds and hearts on what is truly worthy of our attention. Time and time again, we are commanded in Scripture to set our minds—to devote our attention—to particular matters and *not* to others.[12]

As I have previously pointed out, our attention is vital to our moral formation and to the kinds of people we are becoming. Indeed,

---

11. Huggett, *Learning the Language of Prayer*, quoted in Foster and Griffin, *Spiritual Classics*, 11.

12. I recommend that readers pause here and meditatively read 2 Cor. 3:18, Phil. 4:8, and Col. 3:1–2.

according to Gregory of Nyssa, the human soul is created in such a way that it is "shaped in accordance with that which it looks upon."[13] We need, then, to carefully consider the moral shape of our attention precisely because the course of our very lives depends on what we carefully attend to (Col. 3:1–4). We need a virtuous and Christ-shaped "ethics of attention."[14]

Our consideration of the exercise of meditation would not be complete without at least a brief look at an interesting aspect of the ancient conception of philosophy as a way of life, in both its Christian and non-Christian expressions, that involves a wider form of meditation: meditating on death (*memento mori*).[15] While this might sound strange and a bit morbid, the idea of living now in light of our end has deep roots in Scripture and in the Christian philosophical tradition.

In his dialogue *Phaedo*, Plato says that "those who practice philosophy in the right way are in training for dying and they fear death least of all men."[16] As Pierre Hadot points out, this notion of the philosophical life as training and preparation for death is picked up by later Christian thinkers such as Maximus the Confessor (580–662), Clement of Alexandria, and Gregory Nazianzen. "In conformity with the philosophy of Christ," Maximus says, "let us make of our life a training for death."[17]

Since the Christian philosophical life is one that strives to be properly attuned to what is truly real and good in Christ in the present,

13. *Homily on the Song of Songs 5*, in Gregory of Nyssa, *Homilies on the Song of Songs*, 163. I thank Derek King for pointing me to this reference.
14. Crawford, *World beyond Your Head*, 7–8.
15. For evidence of the widespread acceptance of meditating on death as part of a philosophical way of life in antiquity—from Greek, Roman, and Hellenistic sources—see Hadot, *Philosophy as a Way of Life*, 93–101.
16. *Phaedo* 67e, in *Plato: Complete Works*, 59.
17. Maximus the Confessor, *Commentary on the Our Father*, quoted in Hadot, *Philosophy as a Way of Life*, 138.

it will involve the regular exercise of properly meditating on death.[18] From a Christian perspective, meditating on death involves cultivating and maintaining a perspective on the present that is illuminated by and anchored in the life to come. This eternal perspective looks "not to the things that are seen but to the things that are unseen. For the things that are seen are transient, but the things that are unseen are eternal" (2 Cor. 4:18). As we will see in more detail in chapter 10, living philosophically as a Christian means living moment by moment with our final end or *telos* in mind (2 Cor. 5:6–10). In this way, the Christian philosophical life is, from beginning to end, *eschatological*.[19] Living in the present in light of the end reminds us that there are human goods and just causes worth pursuing and standing for—such as seeking and upholding truth and justice—that are far weightier than merely maintaining a pulse. As even Socrates pointed out on the eve of his execution, to lose these weighty moral goods is far worse than physical death.[20]

Spiritual Friendship

Let me close this chapter with a too-often-neglected spiritual *exercise of engagement* that provides one of the strongest remedies for our modern existential ailments: *spiritual friendship*. We noted in chapter 3 that friendship in general played a vital role as a communal spiritual exercise for many philosophical ways of life in antiquity. If we fail to grasp the proper role of friendship in the philosophical life and in the human life well lived, we will inevitably

18. A proper meditation on death is one that is undertaken in the light and grace of Christ, freed from the bondage of a crippling fear of death (Heb. 2:14–15).

19. In *Spiritual Exercises*, Ignatius of Loyola commends meditating on death: "I should picture myself at the hour of my death, and ponder well the way and norm I would then wish to have observed in carrying out the duties of my office" (340).

20. *Apology* 38a–40d, in Plato, *Trial and Death of Socrates*, 40–41.

wander and be lured away by false visions of reality and the good life and fail to reach our God-appointed destination. This is precisely why the exercise of cultivating spiritual friendships is a truth-directed practice that is essential for living philosophically *as a Christian.*

The exercise of spiritual friendship is the practice of cultivating enduring and virtuous friendships with others—friendships that are rooted in and founded on a common life in Christ—for the sake of living well.[21] Let's slow down and consider several important ideas that stand at the heart of the nature and value of spiritual friendship: the nature of human beings in general, the nature of friendship in general, and the essential role of spiritual friendship for living well in Christ.

First, a point about *what* we are as human beings. Aristotle rightly pointed out that humans are "political animals," not in the sense that we crave savvy party politics but in the sense that we are the kinds of creatures that naturally and freely form social groups such as families, societies, governments, nations, and so on. As Aristotle put it, "A human being is a political animal that tends by nature to live together with others."[22] This is a point about what we are by nature and what we are primed to strive for, not about what we just happen to prefer or desire. Just as a plant tends *by nature* to put down roots to draw nourishment from the surrounding soil, so too human beings *by nature* tend to put down relational roots to draw soul nourishment from their surrounding social environment.

Second, a point about the various types of friendship in our common life together. Again, Aristotle hit the nail on the head when he identified three different types of friendship: *friendships of utility,*

---

21. For an excellent older treatment of spiritual friendship, see Rievaulx, *Spiritual Friendship*. For a noteworthy contemporary discussion of spiritual friendship, see Chan, *Spiritual Theology*, chap. 9.

22. Aristotle, *Nicomachean Ethics* 9.9, 1169b20, p. 176.

friendships of pleasure, and *friendships of virtue.*[23] *Friendships of utility* are built solely on the basis of mutual benefit. These kinds of friendships are valuable "not insofar as the beloved is who he is, but insofar as he is useful or pleasant." We value friends of utility solely because of what they can do for *us*, not because of who they are in themselves. So a business colleague, a fellow student in your Introduction to Philosophy class, and a coach are all common examples of friendships of utility. Friendships of utility are, as Aristotle recognized, constantly changing and are very fragile and easily dissolved, "for if someone is no longer pleasant or useful, the other stops loving him."[24]

Friendships of pleasure are those that are built solely upon "shared pleasures" and are, according to Aristotle, the type of friendships that are most common among "young people," as he puts it. Since what we judge as pleasurable frequently changes with time, friendships of pleasure also tend to come and go and are not normally stable or enduring through time. Today the very notion of "friendship" has been flattened out and reduced to a spectator-like posture toward the online presence of another, one that begins with the click of a button and can end just as easily. We could identify many if not most of our "digital friends" as either friends of utility or friends of pleasure; we "love" them solely for the sake of mutual benefit or shared pleasure within a digital environment. Such friendships are short-lived and brittle—they easily break when pressed.

Friendships of virtue are the last and most important type of friendship—what Aristotle calls "complete friendship." Virtuous friendship is built on the cultivation of virtuous character (both moral and intellectual) and mutual care for others *for their own sake* and not simply for the sake of utility or pleasure. Aristotle famously described

---

23. Aristotle, *Nicomachean Ethics* 8.3, 1156a7–1156b33, pp. 143–45.
24. Aristotle, *Nicomachean Ethics* 8.3.2, 1156a16–20, p. 143.

one's virtuous friends as *other selves*: "The excellent person is related to his friend in the same way as he is related to himself, since a friend is another himself."[25] For virtuous friends, the well-being of the one is the well-being of the other; each has an abiding commitment to and a vested interest in the other's moral and intellectual formation and ability to live well and wisely in the world. Aristotle notes that virtuous friendships take a lot of time to cultivate and are rarely encountered. Yet he thought that the effort was well worth it, because only friendships of this third kind can shape our lives around the true, the good, and the beautiful.

And now the point about the role of friendship in living well, ultimately in Christ: Aristotle thought that "anyone who is to be happy, then, will need excellent friends," and he was spot on.[26] In fact, many classical Christian thinkers, such as Augustine and Aquinas, drew upon (and even transposed into a higher, Christian key) many of these insights about human nature and friendship to underscore the supreme value of virtuous friendship for living the good life in Christ, which includes living philosophically as a Christian.[27] In fact, Augustine went so far as to say that, given our nature as social creatures, it is *impossible* to truly live the happy life—what he aptly called the life of "joy based on the truth"[28]—without virtuous friendships. Augustine said, "In this world two things are essential: a healthy life and friendship," and "What is there to console us in this human society so full of errors and trials except the truth and mutual love of true and good friends?"[29] Thomas Aquinas also recognized the importance of a social life based on virtue for the pursuit of wisdom

25. Aristotle, *Nicomachean Ethics* 9.9.10, 1170b7–10, p. 177.
26. Aristotle, *Nicomachean Ethics* 9.9.10, 1170b15–20, p. 178.
27. See Burt, *Friendship and Society*; and Schwartz, *Aquinas on Friendship*.
28. Augustine, *Confessions* 10.23, p. 199.
29. Augustine, "Sermon 299D" and *City of God* 19.8, quoted in Burt, *Friendship and Society*, 57–58.

and truth as well as rightly ordered action when he said, "Whether in the works of the active life, or in those of the contemplative life, [one] needs the fellowship of friends."[30]

Virtuous friends mutually encourage one another to stay the course of the true and the good and thus divert one another's attention from "worthless things" (Ps. 119:37). Viewed with the ailing eyes of our modern, pragmatically oriented world, "friendship is unnecessary, like philosophy, like art, like the universe itself," said C. S. Lewis, and "it has no survival value; rather it is one of those things which give value to survival."[31] Consequently, in enabling us to keep our gaze fixed on the true and our will fastened to the good, the practice of cultivating virtuous friendships is a *truth-directed* exercise and thus relevant to the Christian *philosophical* way of life.

Spiritual friendship is a certain kind of virtuous friendship. Spiritual friendships provide the essential relational connections to others by which we learn to love and be loved, primarily by those who are connected to us not by blood but by the Spirit. While spiritual friendship includes a mutual regard for the cultivation of each other's moral and intellectual character, its roots draw nourishment from a deeper soil than this, we might say. Spiritual friends share a common bond of the Spirit and thus together draw on the Spirit's live-giving resources to sustain them on life's journey. They share their lives in the hope that they might mutually sharpen one another (Prov. 27:17) "until Christ is formed" in them (Gal. 4:19).

Since spiritual friendships are built on a common life that rests on the firmest of foundations (Matt. 7:24–27), they are deeply committed, stable, and enduring; they do not break apart when the circumstances of life press on them. Indeed, Scripture clearly distinguishes a *companion* from a *spiritual friend* in this way (Prov. 18:24). The

---

30. Thomas Aquinas, *Summa theologiae* I-II, q. 4, art. 8, pp. 54–55.
31. Lewis, *Four Loves*, 103.

difference between the two is one of degree of commitment: companions will likely cut and run at the earliest sign of inconvenience, but spiritual friends will stick "closer than a brother." Thus, spiritual friends are deeply committed to helping each other see and live along the grain of reality as it is in Christ, even in the face of great personal and social risk, all for the sake of helping each other see and savor God in truth, goodness, and beauty.

Of course, as with virtuous friendships in general, spiritual friendships will take a great deal of time to cultivate and will be few, at least on this side of eternity. But the effort is well worth it, since without spiritual friends our vision of reality and the good life will become distorted, and our wayward loves will lead us away from the "good way" where we find rest for our souls (Jer. 6:16).

Examples of Christian Spiritual Exercises and Their Therapeutic Benefits

Spiritual Exercises for a Christian Philosophical Way of Life	Meaning	Remedies for Our Existential Ailments
Solitude and Silence	The spiritual exercises of purposefully abstaining from social interaction and communication with others for the sake of realigning our wayward heart and mind to God's kingdom purposes (Matt. 14:13, 23; Mark 6:31; Luke 5:16).	*Channel*: the regular practice of solitude and silence can enable a greater openness and responsiveness to God and the true, the good, and the beautiful. *Corrective*: the regular practice of solitude and silence can help correct disordered patterns of social life, including an unhealthy need to seek one's identity and value in the approval of others over and above the pursuit of wisdom. *Preventative*: the regular practice of solitude and silence can help prevent the love of empty and vain spectacle and other distorted patterns of social life.
Self-Examination and Meditation	*Self-Examination*: the spiritual exercise of inviting God's loving presence to search and sift our mind and heart and to lead us in the way of flourishing in Christ (Ps. 139:23–24; 1 Cor. 11:28; Phil. 1:9–10; Col. 1:9). *Meditation*: the spiritual exercise of cultivating a greater awareness of God's presence through prayerfully attending to his written word with the guidance of the Holy Spirit (Ps. 119:15, 23, 48).	*Channel*: the regular practice of meditation and self-examination can enable a greater awareness of who we really are, who we are becoming, and who God intends for us to be in Christ. *Corrective*: the regular practice of meditation and self-examination can help reveal and correct false and life-denying visions of reality and the good life when we wander from the "good way" (Jer. 6:16). *Preventative*: the regular practice of meditation and self-examination can guard against self-deception, excessive visual noise, and becoming acclimated to an overly polluted information landscape.

Spiritual Exercises for a Christian Philosophical Way of Life	Meaning	Remedies for Our Existential Ailments
Spiritual Friendship	The spiritual exercise of cultivating and keeping friendships that are rooted in the common bond of the Spirit and marked by a mutual regard for the moral, intellectual, and spiritual formation of the other until "Christ is formed in them" (Prov. 18:24; 27:17; Gal. 4:19; Phil. 1:27–28; 4:3).	*Channel*: the regular practice of cultivating and keeping spiritual friendships can empower us to clearly see and steadily walk with and not against the grain of reality—what is ultimately true and good in Christ—in the face of rival secular narratives, misinformation, and social pressures. *Corrective*: spiritual friendships can facilitate regular mind's-eye and heart exams and lovingly but firmly guide us to the needed soul-therapy to mend our wayward condition. *Preventative*: spiritual friendships can help divert our attention away from "worthless things" (Ps. 119:37) and recalibrate us to what is true, good, and beautiful in Christ.
Existential Rest	The spiritual exercise of honoring God by regularly living in alignment with our God-given creaturely limitations, through the cultivation of restful life-rhythms (Ps. 131; Jer. 17:5–8).	*Channel*: the regular practice of existential rest keeps us tethered to the reality of who we truly are as finite, limited creatures of God and keeps us rightly attuned to the God-ordained moral grain of reality. *Corrective*: existential rest helps reorder our minds and hearts when ailed by existential vertigo and our sinful tendency to try to overstep our God-given creaturely limits (i.e., the Promethean ideal). *Preventative*: existential rest can help guard against self-deception, an overinflated view of ourselves, and our sinful tendency to find our identity and worth in what we *do* rather than who we *are* in Christ.

7

Philosophy for the Sake of What, Exactly?

Introducing Practicality Questions

"How in the world is philosophy even remotely practical? How can this possibly help with making a living, let alone with evangelism, discipleship, and ministry?" These are the questions I get more than any others, both in the classroom and in everyday conversations about the study of philosophy. I've now accepted the fact that they simply come with the territory of teaching philosophy at an evangelical seminary.

Let's refer to questions of this general type as *practicality questions*. While practicality questions come in many shapes and sizes, they all share an underlying concern: What does philosophizing have to do with how I should live—in particular, how I should live the Christian life? Please don't get me wrong at the outset: practicality questions are important questions to ask of any rightly formed

Christian intellectual inquiry, one that is not inordinately turned inward but properly ordered outward to the health and integrity of the people of God and to the advancement of God's mission in the world. Yet, more often than not, behind well-meaning practicality questions lurk a host of unstated and deeply entrenched (often unbiblical) assumptions about the nature of human beings, about value and the kinds of goals worth seeking, and about the nature of Christian ministry and its relation to the intellectual life. And lurkers need to be brought into the light.

In the rest of this book, I'll introduce and critically interact with the following four assumptions that tend to hide behind practicality questions:

- Philosophy is good for nothing (chap. 7).
- If an activity or pursuit is valuable, it's valuable only for the sake of something else (chap. 7).
- An activity is "practical" only if it produces useful, measurable outcomes (chap. 8).
- The Christian life and ministry have nothing to do with the philosophical life and the cultivation of the intellect (chaps. 9–10).

As you will see, each of these assumptions smuggles in some heavy-duty philosophical and theological commitments about what we are as humans and what is and isn't valuable and practical for human life and flourishing in Christ.

Hidden Assumption No. 1: Philosophy Is Good for Nothing

A first possible motivating assumption lurking behind practicality questions, one that I find to be less common than it used to be, is that *philosophy is good for nothing* or that *philosophical inquiry has no value whatsoever for the Christian*. At best, philosophical reflection is simply seen as a waste of time; at worst, it is understood as positively harmful to vibrant Christian faith and discipleship. Practicality questions in this vein are often raised because many struggle to see the relevance and practicality of deep, sustained intellectual reflection on the nature of reality, truth, science, knowledge, value, human beings, and so forth. After all, philosophical reflection is hard and can seem very far removed from ordinary matters of human concern. How might reflecting deeply on the nature of reality, truth, knowledge, and value even remotely bear on reaching my coworkers for Christ?

These are valid concerns that need to be taken seriously by the Christian philosopher. It is important to point out first that this assumption—that philosophical inquiry has no value whatsoever for the Christian—harbors substantive convictions about value: in particular, what activities are valuable and worth pursuing for the Christian. The irony, of course, is that these convictions are at root *philosophical* convictions. But let's leave that deep tension aside for now because, ironic as it may be, some of the other hidden assumptions also smuggle in substantive philosophical commitments.

More importantly, when I hear this underlying assumption ring out in the subtext of a student's practicality question (often supported by a passing mention of Colossians 2:8, without attention to its proper context), I no longer immediately feel the need to go all out in defense of the importance and value of philosophy for Christian discipleship, formation, and mission. I no longer see these occasions as invitations to hastily try to justify my existence as a philosopher at the Christian intellectual table. I have seen that, more often than not, the question stems from a deficiency of firsthand experience wrestling with the big questions and with how they connect with some of the deepest longings of the human heart. In my experience, the student has never actually been shown *how* philosophy, both as a subject and as an activity, bears on, informs, guides, and governs matters of grave human concern such as the reality and nature of God, the human soul, freedom, identity, destiny, value, meaning, purpose, and so forth. They have never witnessed the Christian philosophical life lived out, we might say. I can't help but think that those in this camp have either never directly encountered philosophy or, if they have, that some prior philosophy teacher failed them somewhere along the way (just as my first philosophy professor failed to even attempt to connect philosophy with deep human concerns).

I now extend a simple invitation to such a student: "Come and see for yourself." I invite these students into a kind of intellectual dance, to join me in a posture of wonder about the marvelous reality that God has made and the perennial and enduring questions at the heart of human existence. Then, after we finish dancing, I invite them to decide for themselves whether philosophical inquiry is at all valuable and whether living philosophically as a Christian is as bad as they once thought. More often than not, they find that they really do like to dance (yes, even the Baptist students!) and that carefully and honestly wrestling with the perennial questions brings in its wake a kind of intellectual sure-footedness, a deep-seated stability and maturity that may be valuable for the Christian life, discipleship, and mission after all (Eph. 4:11–16).

Hidden Assumption No. 2: If an Activity or Pursuit Is Valuable, It's Valuable Only for the Sake of Something Else

A second possible assumption lurking behind practicality questions is that in order for an activity or pursuit to be valuable or worthwhile, it must contribute to the value of some other activity. In the case at hand, philosophical inquiry—perhaps intellectual inquiry more broadly—is valuable or worth pursuing purely for the sake of something else: for instance, a passing grade, a college degree, evangelism, serving as theology's handmaiden, counseling, missions, or ministry in general. Whatever value philosophical thinking might bring in its wake, it is most definitely not worth pursuing *for its own sake*. After all, haven't we all heard the common trope about philosophers sitting in their ivory towers and navel-gazing? Haven't we been duly warned that those who are too heavenly minded are of no earthly good?

This second assumption undergirding practicality questions is not often explicitly stated in polite company, but very often it rears its head when someone places importance on deep, hard, and sustained reflection about the nature of the true, the good, and the beautiful and on the cultivation of one's God-given mind *for its own sake*. Few take issue with the apostle Paul for conversing with pagan philosophers on Mars Hill, for studying and quoting pagan sources from memory, when this clearly aided in the task of evangelism and gospel-witness. But red flags are quickly raised, and charges of undue speculation abound, when the acquisition of truth and knowledge about reality are prized for their own sake and valued as truly fulfilling in themselves. However well-intentioned, this common knee-jerk reaction fails to acknowledge the deep strain of biblical teaching concerning the intrinsic value of truth, knowledge, wisdom, and virtue as indispensable aspects of a full, flourishing human life (Prov. 2; Phil. 4:8; 2 Pet. 1:5–11).[1]

Philosophers, at least since the time of Plato, have distinguished between two types of value: *instrumental value* and *intrinsic value*.[2] Some activity is instrumentally valuable when it is valuable because it helps us achieve something else of value. Saving money, for example,

---

1. For an excellent treatment of the intrinsic value of the intellectual life, see Hitz, *Lost in Thought*.
2. See *Republic* 2, 357a–359c, in *Plato: Complete Works*, 998–1000.

is arguably valuable insofar as it helps us achieve some further valuable goal, such as greater financial stability or an education; the value of saving money is linked to its ability to help achieve some further valuable end. On the other hand, something—say a human being or an artistic masterpiece—is intrinsically valuable if it is valuable *for its own sake*. Human beings are valuable for their own sake, as ends in themselves, and should not be used or treated as mere means to an end.

Practicality questions motivated by this second hidden assumption fail to see that not *all* value can be instrumental; indeed, some activities must be truly fulfilling *in themselves* and thus worthy of pursuing *for their own sake*. Why think this? A quick but long-standing philosophical argument aims to make this very point. We can think about this in terms of stepping stones. Stepping stones are beneficial only because they ultimately help us get somewhere that is not another stepping stone (e.g., the bank on the other side of the river). If *every* stone were a mere stepping stone, then our efforts to reach an end point by way of stepping stones would prove futile. We would be forever hopping from one stone to another without ever arriving at the place to which the stepping stones are meant to lead us. Unless the stepping stones ultimately bring us to an end point that is itself not another stepping stone, we would be right to suspect that stepping stones are ultimately good for nothing.

In the same way, Aristotle argued that if *every* action is pursued for the sake of some other valuable goal or outcome, then this "will go on without limit, so that desire will prove to be empty and futile."[3] That is, if I carry out action *A* (getting a job) for the sake of some good *B* (acquiring money), and if I carry out *B* for the sake of *C* (paying rent), and if I carry out *C* for the sake of *D* (not getting evicted), and so on indefinitely without ever reaching a goal worth valuing

---

3. Aristotle, *Nicomachean Ethics* 1.2, p. 1.

for its own sake, then one would be right to question whether *A*, *B*, *C*, or *D* are even instrumentally valuable in the first place. As with the stepping stones, unless these valuable pursuits ultimately bring us to an end point that is good for its own sake and not pursued for the sake of anything else, we might begin to doubt whether *A–D* are ultimately good for *anything*. If this little argument is right (and I encourage you to try it on and see whether it fits), then there must be some activities or pursuits that are *intrinsically* valuable (good for their own sake) and whose merits are not found in some good beyond them; such activities and ends are their own reward, we might say.

Against the backdrop of the hustle and bustle of our excessively pragmatic and success-oriented culture (which sadly encompasses a great deal of Christian culture as well), this truth alone is startling and should awaken us to the question of what these intrinsically valuable ends and pursuits might be. As we live and move and have our being in our modern age, many of us have become habituated into thinking that something is valuable only if it furthers one's career, social status, social media platform, academic standing, reputation, religious accomplishment, preaching ability, bank account, or whatever. Many of us struggle mightily with the idea that devoting ourselves to the cultivation of our God-given natural capacities (whether physical, intellectual, moral, or aesthetic) is valuable *for its own sake* (friendship, play, exercise, art, good conversation, reading, music, etc.).

From my experience with this underlying assumption in the classroom, I think the problem more often than not has to do with the struggle to see the intrinsic value of the *intellectual life* in particular. We don't think to question the intrinsic value of cultivating and forming our moral characters, devoting ourselves to the acquisition of moral virtues and the uprooting of deep-seated moral vices. Few would push back on the assumption that becoming the kind of person we morally ought to be is valuable for its own sake; of course it is!

But, for some reason or other, things are just flat-out different when it comes to the intellectual life.

We can quickly grant that *inordinate* devotion to the intellectual life at the expense of other important goods (such as caring for those in need in one's immediate community and being a godly and attentive mother or father, a loving and faithful friend, a devoted spouse, an active local church member, etc.) would also be to miss the mark completely.[4] But ask yourself this: Is there really a relevant difference in value between the cultivation of one's *moral character* and the cultivation of one's *intellectual character*? Are not *both* moral capacities and intellectual capacities God-given capacities that belong to the *entire* human person, created in the image of God? If cultivating a rightly ordered will toward the good is valuable for its own sake, why would cultivating a rightly ordered mind toward the true not be valuable for its own sake as well? Why pit one set of natural, God-given human capacities against the other with regard to their intrinsic value? And if there *is* a radical difference in intrinsic value, what could possibly explain it?

On reflection, it is much more plausible to think that the cultivation of *all* one's natural capacities in the direction of what is truly good and fulfilling for humans as designed by God is *both* intrinsically *and* instrumentally valuable.[5] We were created with (at least) two deep, metaphysical hungers, one for moral goodness and another for truth, each corresponding to the unique, God-given human capacity of will and intellect. Indeed, "man is, to the very roots of his being, a creature designed for and desiring vision."[6]

---

4. For more on the concept of the inordinate and thus immoral shape of the intellectual life, see Inman, "Epistemic Temperance."

5. See 2 Pet. 1:3–12 for a nice example of how the acquisition and cultivation of moral "qualities" (1:9–12) pertaining to the intellect and will is *both* intrinsically *and* instrumentally valuable for the flourishing life in Christ.

6. "Earthly Contemplation," in *Josef Pieper: An Anthology*, 143.

Thus, as I pointed out in chapter 2 where I described philosophizing as a uniquely human activity and way of life, there turns out to be a deep theological and philosophical reason for why the philosophical life is *intrinsically valuable*. The reason is this: *you are human*. If humans are meaning-seeking animals by nature, then philosophical activity should be thought of not as an optional aid to a human life well lived but rather as an essential ingredient to the distinctively human life well lived. There's a clear difference between lemons as an *optional add-on* to lemonade and lemons as an *essential ingredient* for lemonade: the lemons are the very things that make the drink lemonade and not apple juice. Likewise, there's a clear difference between a baseball as an *optional add-on* to a baseball game and a baseball as an indispensable and *essential ingredient* of the game: the baseball *itself* is what makes the game a baseball game and not a soccer game.

Similarly, if humans have a God-given, unique hunger for understanding and making meaningful sense of the totality of things and how everything hangs together, then satisfying this appetite (to whatever degree) via a philosophical way of life will be an essential ingredient to *human* flourishing, not an optional add-on. As Josef Pieper says, "'The good of man,' and a meaningful human existence, consists, as far as possible, in seeing things as they are, and in living and acting in accordance with the truth thus apprehended. . . . Thus man's chief nourishment is truth. This does not apply only to the man of knowledge, the philosopher, the scientist. Anyone who wishes to live a truly human life must feed on truth."[7] So, at bottom, the question of whether philosophical activity is intrinsically valuable in any way or just merely instrumentally valuable cannot be answered apart from the wider philosophical question of what human beings *are* and what their God-given capacities are *for*. And it is precisely

7. "The Defense of Freedom," in *Josef Pieper: An Anthology*, 123–24.

because of *what* we are by nature—meaning-seeking animals who naturally hunger for truth and the wonder of it all—that the fulfillment of these natural human capacities is valuable for its own sake.[8] Yet we need not denigrate the instrumental value of philosophy to underscore the main point here that Christian philosophical inquiry—and the Christian philosophical life in general—can be valuable *for its own sake*. By no means! A well-cultivated philosophical mind, and walking in a Christian philosophical way of life more generally, is incredibly valuable for evangelism and Christian witness, particularly in our post-Christian age in which the Christian Way (Acts 9:2) is widely contested and no longer seen as a live option on the cultural table.[9] Even more, I'm convinced that cultivating the life of the mind by way of philosophical reflection can be an act of loving service to the church, especially for those who are graced with the gift of teaching the body of Christ for the sake of intellectual and spiritual maturity (Eph. 4:1–16).

At bottom, once we see that not *all* value is instrumental, we are no longer required to choose between ascribing mere instrumental value to philosophy alone or ascribing no value to it at all. Rather, truly fulfilling human activities such as living philosophically can be *both* valuable for their own sake *and* valuable for the sake of some further valuable goal or end.

---

8. On this important point related to philosophical anthropology, see Pieper, *Only the Lover Sings*, 21–22; and Pieper, *Happiness and Contemplation*, 58–61. Moreover, David McPherson has an excellent treatment of this connection in McPherson, *Virtue and Meaning*, 166–80.

9. On this point, see Taylor, *Secular Age*; and Newbigin, *Foolishness to the Greeks*.

8

Philosophy Is Practical?
Are You Kidding?

Hidden Assumption No. 3: An Activity Is "Practical" Only If It Produces Useful, Measurable Outcomes

A third possible motivating assumption behind practicality questions involves *the nature of the practical itself.* Let's briefly pause and reflect on why it is so jarring to our contemporary ears to hear that living philosophically as a Christian may be one of the most practical ways you could possibly live your life.

Much of the information that we take in is processed against the backdrop of the vast number of things we take ourselves to already know about the world—what philosophers call "background knowledge." When I'm told that the cheese is old and moldy, I process this bit of information against the backdrop of my *preexisting* knowledge about what cheese and mold are and whether mold on cheese is to be desired or not. In precisely the same way, we hear the above statement

about the practicality of philosophy against the backdrop of our *pre-existing* knowledge of what it means to be "practical" and "relevant."
And here is where we need to slow down and try to shed some light on our shared cultural background knowledge concerning what it means to be "practical" and "relevant" in the first place. The reality is that our current cultural environment—both inside and outside the church—harbors and even champions a particular view about which activities are practically relevant and which are not. So what exactly is this cultural backdrop that makes philosophical reflection seem so utterly impractical and irrelevant to matters of "real life" and pressing human concern?

The Workaday World and "the Practical"

Perhaps more than any philosopher in recent history, the German Christian philosopher Josef Pieper has devoted careful attention to the nature of the philosophical life and its seeming impracticality relative to contemporary human life.[1] Pieper perceptively identifies what he calls "the workaday world" as the modern cultural backdrop by which we judge whether an activity is considered valuable, practical, or relevant. According to Pieper, the workaday world is dominated and driven by the notions of usefulness, productivity, optimization, and efficiency. In particular, the workaday world claims to offer a clean and easy way to measure value and practicality: if an activity or pursuit is to be considered valuable and worthy of your time and resources and thus practical, it must maximize some economic, measurable outcome or product.

But why, exactly, does the workaday world deem the production of measurable outcomes *the* ultimate standard by which we judge what

---

1. In particular, see Pieper, *Leisure*; Pieper, *Philosophical Act*; Pieper, *In Defense of Philosophy*; Pieper, *For the Love of Wisdom*.

is truly valuable, relevant, and practical to human life? Pieper insightfully argues that the reason is anchored in a deeper, pernicious view of human nature that lies at the heart of the workaday world: "The process of production itself is understood and proclaimed as the activity that gives meaning to human existence."[2] The workaday world breeds a view of what it means to be human that is antithetical to the Christian story: you *are* what you *produce*; the more you produce and have to show for yourself, the more valuable you are. In the popular children's TV show *Thomas & Friends* (featuring Thomas the Tank Engine), the highest compliment that can be paid to a train engine in the land of Sodor is that it is "very useful." In the same way, the highest compliment that can be paid to an activity or a human life in the land of the workaday world is that it is "very useful." We are all Sir Topham Hatt now.[3]

The steady pulse of the workaday world—driven in many ways by the underlying Promethean ideal discussed in chapter 5—is propelled by a deeply impoverished and one-dimensional understanding of human nature and human life in general. In Western society, we generally no longer view our collective human vocation in terms of satisfying our natural hunger for truth, goodness, and beauty, nor do we view our lives as a part of a grand divine drama. As a result, we inevitably substitute "the common need" in the place of "the common good" and are left with productivity, technique, utility, and efficiency as the only reliable means to measure value and to secure the kind of life we *want* rather than the kind of life we truly *need* in virtue of our nature.[4] Pieper insightfully asks, "Can a full human existence be

---

2. Pieper, *Leisure*, 60.
3. Sir Topham Hatt is the fictional character in *Thomas & Friends* who ensures that the railway is run in a way that is maximally productive and efficient and assures each of the train engines that they are valuable only to the extent that they are "very useful." (If you can't already tell, I'm a full-time dad of three little people.)
4. For discussion of the idea of the "common need" versus the "common good," see Pieper, *Philosophical Act*, 78.

contained within an exclusively workaday existence?"[5] If Christianity is true, the answer is crystal clear: no, it cannot.

Interestingly enough, there is both a Christian and a non-Christian version of the workaday world that tends to measure all worthwhile activities in terms of instrumental value and utility. The Christian version of the workaday world is prone to view "progress" in the Christian life and "success" in ministry *solely* in terms of quantifiable, measurable outcomes such as frequent church attendance, the amount of time spent in prayer or daily devotion, the number of evangelistic encounters or professions of faith secured, the number of missionaries sent abroad, the number of engaging and sound sermons delivered, and the like. There is, of course, nothing intrinsically wrong with quantifiable results when they are the organic by-product of genuine health and substance. But, as Jesus himself reminds us (Matt. 5:20; 7:21–27; John 6:60–71), such measurable, quantifiable outcomes alone are in no way indicative of the kind of moral and intellectual maturity that marks genuine Christian discipleship.

As we will see in detail in the next chapter, when the Christian life and ministry are taken up into the whirlwind of the workaday world and instrumentalized in this way, they cease to be anchored in and to orbit around their proper heavenly and contemplative frame. As a result, the full shape of the richness and depth of the Christian life and ministry—in terms of clearly seeing and wisely living along the grain of reality as it is in Christ and helping others to do the same—is either gravely distorted or altogether lost. And, sadly, the downstream consequence of a vison of the Christian life that is misshaped by the workaday world is a Christian faith and mission in the world that is excessively narrow, devoid of power and vitality, and ultimately fruitless (2 Pet. 1:3–15).

5. Pieper, *Leisure*, 39.

The Workaday World and the Uselessness of Philosophy

What then becomes of activities or areas of human creativity that fail to measure up as "useful" or "productive" or "practical" according to the value standards of the workaday world? What happens to poetry, literature, history, the arts, and philosophy in particular against the backdrop of this morally and metaphysically impoverished framework? Well, at best, such areas of inquiry become increasingly sidelined in the public eye; at worst, they become academically extinct and blacklisted from the guild of worthwhile human pursuits. Herein lies the current crisis of the humanities in higher education that is further evidenced by decreased funding for the humanities (in comparison with STEM disciplines) and by the closing of philosophy departments in both Christian and non-Christian colleges and universities across the United States.[6]

Exhibit A here would be the suspicion that many, Christians included, have about the study of the liberal arts and the humanities in particular. In 2015, Florida senator Marco Rubio captured this public sentiment well when he said, "Welders make more money than philosophers. We need more welders and less philosophers."[7] It is thought to be "a waste of time and tuition dollars" to devote oneself to a slow reading of Plato's *Republic* accompanied by rich reflection on the nature of individual and civic justice, on what constitutes a rightly ordered soul and state. Why bother with studying great works

---

6. "Cuts and Threats to Philosophy Programs," *Daily Nous*, accessed January 10, 2023, https://dailynous.com/category/cuts-and-threats-to-philosophy-programs/.
7. I am happy to report that, in a 2018 post on Twitter, Rubio (@marcorubio) indicated that he has since changed his mind about philosophy: "I made fun of philosophy . . . but then I was challenged to study it, so I started reading the stoics. I've changed my view of philosophy. But not on welders. We need both! Vocational training for workers and philosophers to make sense of the world." Twitter, March 28, 2018, 7:48 a.m., https://twitter.com/marcorubio/status/978961956504788994?lang=en. I think Pieper would be proud.

of literature, history, philosophy, and theology when one could study more practical fields such as finance, business, or one of the natural sciences—fields that can really help people live "better lives"?

Along these lines, Christian philosopher Greg Ganssle recounts a notable experience he once had while attending a panel discussion on the nature and value of the humanities. During the concluding time for questions, he recalls a student referencing a recent scientific study about new medical treatments with the potential to reverse certain forms of blindness and asking, "Given that we could be working to help blind people see, why should we consider investing our lives in the humanities?" Ganssle recalls the immediate and insightful response by one of the humanities professors on the panel: "Because we want there to be something worth seeing."[8] Just stop and think about that response: "something *worth* seeing." Amid flashy new medical technologies designed to help restore physical sight, the question remains: Will we retain the ability to *truly* see the world and draw out its hidden richness, meaning, and depth?

The student's question about the practical relevance of deep, substantive engagement with the humanities in the face of real human need is, of course, in no way novel; the question has had many different variations over time. C. S. Lewis, in his sermon "Learning in War-Time"—delivered in October 1939, just a month after Germany invaded Poland, commencing the Second World War—considered the very same type of question: "Given that we are in the midst of Wartime, why should we consider investing our lives in the humanities?" In an explicitly evangelical Christian context, one might hear the following argument: "Given the countless number of people dying each day and destined for eternity apart from Christ, why should we consider investing our lives in the humanities?" Or, in light of the recent global health crisis, one might have heard the following:

8. Quoted in Ganssle, *Our Deepest Desires*, 77–78.

"Given that we are in the midst of a global pandemic, why should we consider investing our lives in the humanities?"[9]

At one level, the questioner is spot on: we *are* faced with real and crushing human need on a daily basis. But, without minimizing the importance of our physical and biological needs as embodied creatures, we can truly say that our greatest, most pressing need as meaning-seeking animals is not first and foremost biological but is the kind of stable health and strength of soul that can be nourished only by a steady diet of the true, the good, and the beautiful.

Yet, against the backdrop of the anemic moral and metaphysical assumptions of the workaday world, this emphasis on living fully human lives and cultivating things worth seeing falls by the wayside. Philosophical activity "inevitably becomes more and more distant, strange, and remote; it even assumes the appearance of an intellectual luxury . . . as the workaday world extends its claims and its sway over man."[10] Against the backdrop of the workaday world, a life devoted to becoming increasingly attuned and receptive to the true, the good, and beautiful in Christ will be viewed, at best, as the optional, luxurious add-on package to human life (like optional leather trim or heated seats in a car) rather than as a standard operating feature of human life (like a steering wheel or tires).[11] At worst, a philosophical way of life will be viewed as utterly useless to human existence and will be actively discouraged both inside and outside the university and the church—unless, of course, it can deliver some measurable result or quantitative outcome (good luck with that!).

Along with other areas of human creativity such as poetry, literature, and the arts, philosophy "transcends the world of work"[12]

9. Cyr and Swenson, "Learning in the Time of the Pandemic."
10. Pieper, *Philosophical Act*, 79.
11. I borrow this illustrative concept from Kevin Vanhoozer in Vanhoozer and Strachan, *Pastor as Public Theologian*, 27.
12. Pieper, *Philosophical Act*, 91.

because it does not derive its value solely from the practical results it produces or the measurable outcomes it secures. In this way, the intrinsic value of living philosophically is "free" in that it resists being purely instrumentalized and put to work in the results-driven economy of the workaday world. For people deeply suspicious of the workaday world and its impoverished way of measuring value and practical relevance, it is "entirely proper and perfectly as it should be: philosophy is of no use."[13]

Yet it is important to point out that the "freedom" of philosophy from the workaday world and its excessively narrow value structure does not pit the philosophical way of life against the value of human work and our God-given mandate to make something of the world. In fact, Pieper is quick to point out that the intrinsic value and freedom of the philosophical way of life "does not, of course, in any way deny or ignore the world of work (indeed it assumes its prior and necessary existence), but it does affirm . . . that a man's real wealth consists, not in satisfying his needs, not in becoming 'the master and owner of nature,' but in seeing what is and the whole of what is, in seeing things not as useful or useless, serviceable or not, but simply as being."[14] Indeed, according to Pieper, the point of leisure in human life—cultivating a receptiveness to reality in mind and heart in all its wonder and satisfying fullness—is to help carve out wider *humanizing* spaces within a narrow one-dimensional world that tends to reduce all human value and worthwhile pursuits to pragmatic or economic considerations.

In a cultural soil that equates the value of a human pursuit or activity with its social utility or pragmatic usefulness, such humanizing pursuits (poetry, philosophy, the arts, etc.) will wither away and

---

13. Heidegger, *Introduction to Metaphysics*, quoted in Pieper, *In Defense of Philosophy*, 41.
14. Pieper, *Philosophical Act*, 92. Here Pieper draws from René Descartes's *Discourse on Method*.

die. Thus, carving out reflective space to pursue truly *human* activities ensures that we preserve the "ability to look beyond the limits of our social and functional station, to contemplate and celebrate the world as such, to become and be that person who is essentially oriented toward the whole of reality."[15] In short, the humanizing pursuits that are dubbed "useless" by the workaday world are the very ones that are needed to satisfy our deepest, God-given appetites for truth, goodness, and beauty and to enable us to live fully *human* lives instead of simply "making it" from 9 a.m. to 5 p.m.

So, for those whose eyes have adjusted to the value system of the workaday world, distinctively humanizing pursuits such as the pursuit of wisdom for living well will look a lot like, well, nothing. Yet there is, as writer and artist Jenny Odell puts it, "a kind of nothing that's necessary for, at the end of the day, doing something."[16] Once we turn our gaze away from the mistaken moral and metaphysical assumptions that animate the framework of the workaday world (a view of what pursuits are valuable and practically relevant and a view of what it means to be human), we can clearly see that it would be wrong to think that an activity that is *useless* is therefore *worthless*. This is precisely because there is, as Pieper notes, "an existential realm in which such categories as 'profit,' 'feasibility,' 'usefulness,' 'efficiency' mean nothing, a realm that nevertheless is indispensable for a truly human existence."[17] In fact, some of the most valuable and worthwhile human pursuits under the sun—such as cultivating a deep well of wisdom and virtue by nourishing your soul on the true, the good, and the beautiful in Christ—are completely useless in this sense and yet are absolutely indispensable to living well in Christ.

15. "Leisure and Its Threefold Opposition," in *Josef Pieper: An Anthology*, 140.
16. Odell, *How to Do Nothing*, 22.
17. "Liberal Arts," in *Josef Pieper: An Anthology*, 112.

The Practical and the Theoretical: Like Oil and Water?

So, then, what exactly does it mean for something or some pursuit to be practical? As one influential and widely used dictionary defines *practical*, a thing or activity is practical if it is "concerned with the actual doing or use of something rather than with theory and ideas."[18] Let me encourage you to pause and ponder this popular definition of *practical*. Do you see anything fishy about it?

Here's the problem with this popular definition: defining (philosophically, no less!) the practical in this way by severing *action* from *ideas*, practice from theory, is deeply wrongheaded. Why, exactly? The mind is like the laser that guides the missile of action to a particular target. Distinctively human action, action that is rational and intentional, is always goal-oriented and thus directed toward particular outcomes or ends. The will, the primary engine of action, without the guidance of the mind is like a speedboat without a steering wheel: there's power aplenty, but the power needs to be properly guided and directed to an appropriate outcome if one is to successfully attain whatever goal is in view. And, just as you'd expect to eventually find a speedboat that's all power and no goal-oriented direction run aground on the rocks, so too you'd expect to eventually find the human life that is exclusively "concerned with the actual doing or use of something rather than with theory and ideas" shipwrecked on the shores of life.

As we've seen, many residents of the workaday world conceive of "the practical" in *strictly* economic and pragmatic terms. Something is practical only if it helps someone make money, land a prestigious and high-paying job, move up the corporate ladder, get good grades, more easily navigate a conversation about the gospel, parent children better, or give more dynamic and engaging sermons. We often

18. *New Oxford American Dictionary*, 2nd ed. (2005), s.v. "practical."

hear those in this camp sharply and proudly pit the practical *against* the theoretical: "I'm a practical person; I don't tend to bother with theory." Again, while this sentiment may not always be stated explicitly, it tends to crop up in the form of questions (e.g., What are you going to do with *that* degree? Why in the world is philosophy *required* for a master of divinity degree?), quizzical glances, or the resolute avoidance of any semblance of thoughtful reflection on life's ultimate questions.

Unfortunately, I've found this pitting of the practical *against* the theoretical, shaped as it is by the philosophical assumptions and existential anxiety that animate the workaday world, to be all too common in Christian circles. My seminary students often report to me the frequency with which they hear the following, no doubt well-meant, words: "I'd be cautious of seminary; all that theoretical knowledge will quickly drain the vibrancy of your faith in Christ." This, of course, assumes that a vibrant faith in Christ has nothing to do with a mature and well-ordered mind (itself a rather *theoretical* idea, don't you think?). *Head knowledge* and *heart knowledge*, whatever these terms mean, are somehow thought to be a zero-sum game—the more you have of the one, the less you necessarily have of the other.

But here's the tricky thing about the practical when it is defined over and against the theoretical and thus exclusively in terms of outward activity: practical activity cannot be an end in itself but must ultimately be for the sake of some nonpractical activity. Let me try to unpack this idea. We don't tend to engage in so-called practical endeavors—paying college tuition, working a full-time job, raising children, ministering to the poor, preaching sermons, and so forth—for their own sake. Rather, we undertake these valuable pursuits with an eye toward the larger moral framework in which they are embedded. We tend to think that the value of these practical pursuits piggybacks on the pursuit of certain kinds of human goods, on behalf of both ourselves and others, that are intrinsically good and valuable *in their own right*. As Pieper points out, "All practical activity, from practice of the ethical virtues to gaining the means of livelihood, serves something other than itself. And this other thing is not practical activity. It is having what is sought after, while we rest content in the results of our active efforts."[19]

We've already seen that not all valuable pursuits can be merely instrumental and solely for the sake of other valuable pursuits; some worthwhile pursuits must be valuable for their own sake insofar as they fulfill our very God-given natures and are thus essential ingredients of the human life well lived. The overarching purpose of practical pursuits—the purpose that we ultimately aim for, as an archer ultimately aims for a target—is to enable us to lay hold of (and help others lay hold of) the morally satisfying and abundant life offered to us in Christ. It is a stable and abundant life without lack—a Psalm 23 kind of life—that we all ultimately seek for ourselves and for others, *by means of* our practical endeavors. What I desire most for my children, say, is not that their material needs may be met but that the deepest appetites of their souls may be satisfied, nourished, and sustained by the one for whom they were made: the triune God.

When we lose sight of the larger theological and philosophical context that gives practical activity its moral rudder and direction, we thereby lose sight of the proper place that practice has in human life. Again, as Pieper so helpfully puts it, "Practice does become meaningless the moment it sees itself as an end in itself. For this means converting what is by nature a servant into a master—with the inevitable result that it no longer serves any useful purpose."[20] To slightly alter something C. S. Lewis said in a similar context: aim at

---

19. "The Defense of Freedom," in *Josef Pieper: An Anthology*, 121.
20. "The Defense of Freedom," in *Josef Pieper: An Anthology*, 122.

intrinsic goods and you will get instrumental goods thrown in; aim only at instrumental goods and you will get neither.[21]

More importantly, I would argue that an understanding of the practical that completely severs practice (action) from theory (ideas) is positively detrimental to a flourishing life in Christ. Why think such a thing? Let me explain. It is arguably impossible to have a properly ordered will (a will directed to what is truly good and flourishing for humans), and thus properly ordered actions, without having at some level and to some degree a properly ordered mind (a mind that grasps what truly is and what is truly good and fulfilling for humans). An arrow will never reach its proper target if the archer is fundamentally mistaken or lacks a clear sense about what to aim at. In the same way, one cannot live well in the truest, biblical sense of the term and be fundamentally mistaken about what truly is and what goals are ultimately worth pursuing.

There are ample biblical examples of the organic connection between rightly ordered *living* and rightly ordered *thinking*. In the book of Hosea, for example, it is interesting to note that a primary reason for God's sharp chastisement of the nation of Israel was a deeply ingrained and disordered pattern of living that flowed from a disordered pattern of thinking, beginning with the priests of Israel and trickling down to the nation as a whole. Note the organic connection between disordered thinking and disordered living: "Hear the word of the LORD, O children of Israel, for the LORD has a controversy with the inhabitants of the land. There is no faithfulness or steadfast love, and no knowledge of God in the land; there is swearing, lying, murder, stealing, and committing adultery; they break all bounds, and bloodshed follows bloodshed. . . . My people are destroyed for lack of knowledge; because you have rejected knowledge, I reject you from being a priest to me" (Hosea 4:1–2, 6). At bottom, the nation of

21. Lewis, *Mere Christianity*, 134.

Israel's spiritual waywardness and idolatrous practices were rooted, in part, in the people's failure to properly grasp and willfully orient their lives to *the nature of reality*—namely, that the Holy One of Israel alone is the fundamental source of all reality distinct from himself and is exclusively worthy of worship.[22]

This same point—the inseparable and organic connection between properly ordered actions and a properly ordered mind—is made by the apostle Paul in several places throughout the New Testament. In Romans 1:18–32, perhaps one of the most striking and vivid texts illustrating this point, Paul clearly points out the organic relationship between disordered thinking (what he describes as "futile" thinking and a "debased mind") and disordered living. Paul says, "Therefore God gave them up in the lusts of their hearts to impurity, to the dishonoring of their bodies among themselves, *because* they exchanged the truth about God for a lie and worshiped and served the creature rather than the Creator, who is blessed forever! Amen" (vv. 24–25).

Likewise, in the Pastoral Epistles, Paul highlights the living, organic connection between sound *ideas* (theory) and sound *living* (practice). In fact, the word Paul uses to qualify "doctrine" throughout the Pastoral Epistles (1 Tim. 6:3; 2 Tim. 1:13; 4:3; Titus 1:9, 13; 2:1–2)—namely, "sound" (*hygiainō*)—is a medical term meant to convey the health-giving quality of rightly ordered ideas or teaching.[23] A truth-oriented way of life is, for Paul, therapeutic and leads to a greater health of soul. Along these same lines, Paul admonishes Timothy, "If anyone teaches a different doctrine and does not agree with the sound words of our Lord Jesus Christ and the *teaching that*

---

22. On this point, I'd recommend reading and rereading Willard, *Knowing Christ Today*.

23. In his commentary on the Pastoral Epistles, New Testament scholar Robert Gundry translates "sound doctrine" as "healthful teaching," quoted in Vanhoozer, *Hearers and Doers*, 207.

accords with godliness, he is puffed up with conceit and understands nothing" (1 Tim. 6:3–4).

Did you catch that? There are ideas and patterns of thinking that animate godly living, and there are ideas and patterns of thinking that animate ungodly living (Col. 2:8). Time and time again, Paul contrasts ideas about the nature of reality that edify and are life-giving with ideas that are destructive and soul-destroying. In 1 Timothy 1:8–11, Paul describes a host of disordered actions and behaviors that mark those who are "ungodly and sinners," such as murder, sexual immorality, enslavement, lying, and perjury, as "contrary to sound doctrine, in accordance with the gospel of the glory of the blessed God with which I have been entrusted." Note carefully what Paul is saying here: it is health-destroying *patterns of action* or *ways of living* that are in opposition to health-giving *ideas*. Paul's words here make no sense whatsoever if actions and ideas are not intricately and inseparably woven together in human life.

Ideas that properly correspond to the reality of God in Christ enable the saints to be "sound [healthy] in the faith" (Titus 1:13), which is contrasted with having "swerved from the truth" (2 Tim. 2:18; see also 1 Tim. 6:21) and consequently having "made shipwreck of their faith" (1 Tim. 1:19) and indulged "an unhealthy craving for controversy and for quarrels about words, which produce envy, dissension, slander, evil suspicions, and constant friction among people who are depraved in mind and deprived of the truth" (1 Tim. 6:4–5). The inseparability of action and ideas is clear in the mind of the apostle Paul.

For Paul, if the eyes of the heart, so to speak, are routinely fixed on and enthralled by false visions of reality and of the good and flourishing life (visions that idolize power, money, sex, status, pleasure), it will be nearly impossible to "take hold of that which is truly life" (1 Tim. 6:19). An example might help. If you firmly believe that your luggage is the hot-pink Samsonite suitcase when it is not, you will be unable to take hold of that which is truly your luggage when it comes around on the airport baggage carousel. Similarly, if you firmly believe that financial gain is the highest good worth seeking (the summum bonum, as medieval philosophers would put it), then you will be *unable* to take hold of the "one pearl of great value" (Matt. 13:46) and the great "treasure hidden in a field" (Matt. 13:44).

It may well be the case that this is what is going on when Jesus says, "For *it is easier* for a camel to go through the eye of a needle than for a rich person to enter the kingdom of God" (Luke 18:25) and "Whoever does not bear his own cross and come after me *cannot be my disciple*" (Luke 14:27). I think Jesus's point in these two passages is roughly this: those who believe to their core that their wealth or their own desires, needs, and concerns are of ultimate importance in life simply will not be capable of laying hold of "that which is truly life" when it is offered to them: namely, costly apprenticeship to Jesus and inviting others into this reality as well. (This is ultimately why the story of the rich young ruler is so tragic.) If both of your hands are firmly clenched around idols, you will be without an open hand to reach out and lay hold of what truly matters in life.

In the end, the claim that something can be practical in the best sense of the word—in the sense of rightly ordered action—without reference to ideas or the theoretical is utterly untenable, both philosophically and biblically. The truth remains that our ideas (our beliefs in particular) are the rails upon which the train of our lives runs. We ignore at our own peril the inseparable connection between action (practice) and ideas (theory).

The fact is that the flourishing life in Christ, the life that is properly oriented to reality in all its Christ-shaped dimensions (Prov. 8:22–36; Col. 1:15–17), depends on a dynamic interplay between the mind, the will, and rightly ordered actions. A rich inner life—with a well-ordered heart and mind that are oriented toward the good and the true—is the only nutrient-rich soil out of which well-ordered action can grow. This very ancient truth about the inseparability of the intellectual and volitional capacities of human beings was understood by non-Christian and Christian thinkers alike, by Plato and Aristotle and by Augustine and Aquinas (and others)—and by Jesus himself.

Jesus affirmed this inseparability of the mind, the heart, and action when he said, "How can you speak good, when you are evil? For out of the abundance of the heart the mouth speaks. The good person out of his good treasure brings forth good, and the evil person out of his evil treasure brings forth evil" (Matt. 12:34–35). And part of this "good treasure" within a person that brings forth good, no doubt, includes the intellectual dimension of the person (given how the heart is to be understood biblically).[24]

If we lay aside these popular, albeit deeply misguided, ways of characterizing the nature of the practical as either in tension with the theoretical or understood in purely economic and pragmatic terms, what are we to put in their place? In his book *Philosophy for Dummies*, Tom Morris offers a simple but helpful alternative framework: "What is it for something to be practical? Something is practical if it helps you realize your goals. If your goals include knowing who you really are, what life in this world is all about, and what's ultimately important, then philosophy is eminently practical. If these things are not among your goals, well, then you need new goals."[25]

Note that according to this characterization of the practical, practicality is neither praiseworthy nor blameworthy *in and of itself*. Being deceptive, for example, could be exceedingly practical in this sense, insofar as it helps someone achieve the goal of concealing an adulterous relationship. As I tell my students, in this narrow sense, "being practical" is a bit like "being successful": one can be successful at many different things, good and bad, from cultivating virtuous

---

24. See Saucy, *Minding the Heart*.
25. Morris, *Philosophy for Dummies*, 335.

character and achieving financial goals to becoming addicted to co-
caine and avoiding lawful arrest.

We might say, then, that something is practical, *in the best and
most fitting sense of the word*, if it helps one realize *the kinds of goals
ultimately worth seeking*. What kinds of goals are ultimately worth
seeking, and how do we know what those goals are? Upon simple
reflection, it is clear to most that some goals are more worthy of their
time, energy, and devotion than others. Collecting seashells (sorry,
Bob and Penny!), memorizing phonebooks (remember those?), and
counting as high as one can are clearly (clearly!) not as worthy of our
devotion as increasing in knowledge and love of God and neighbor.

So how are we to reliably tell which goals are ultimately valuable
and worth pursuing over others? There's simply no other way to make
progress here except by slowing down and thinking really hard about
it for yourself (perhaps in the company of like-minded, spiritual
friends). Yes, it really is that simple. Careful philosophical and theological reflection on matters of ultimate importance—what exists,
who we are, why we are here, where we are going, what we should
love, and the kind of person we truly ought to be (with the dual lights
of Scripture and sound reason as our guides)—is the tried-and-true
way to gain knowledge about which pursuits are most valuable and
ultimately worth seeking and which pursuits are not. This is nothing
other than the philosophical way of life, the "examined human life,"
as Socrates famously called it.[26]

There is no app that will do this kind of life-altering investigation
for us. Simply installing the latest update will not sharpen our hazy
existential sight and point us to the kind of life truly worth living in all
its fullness. Cultivating a deeper understanding of the metaphysical
and moral contours of reality (and subsequently orienting one's life
to them) is a journey that takes time, patience, courage and resolve,

---

26. *Apology* 38a, in Plato, *Trial and Death of Socrates*, 40.

a lot of human effort in the company of spiritual friends, and even greater portions of divine grace each step of the way. Thinking well about life is hard; living well is even harder. There are no shortcuts. But we don't have to go it alone, and the effort is more than worth it!

For the Christian, the life of wisdom and *shalom*, the life lived along the grain of reality in all its beauty and delight, properly oriented to the triune God and all that is true, good, and beautiful, is the chief goal of human existence—the one that is worth seeking above all others (Prov. 2; 8:32–36; Jer. 17:5–8). What could be more practical, biblically speaking, than a mind that has cultivated the ability to clearly see, with twenty-twenty existential vision, the best and the highest goals of human life? So, to echo Tom Morris's remark above, if our ultimate goal is to live a life that is properly oriented to God and neighbor in truth and love, then it's hard to see what could be *more* practical than living philosophically as a Christian. The Christian philosophical way of life helps us identify which goals are ultimately worthy of pursuit, and it subsequently helps us orient our actions to successfully lay hold of them. And, if a life properly oriented to God and neighbor in truth and love is *not* an ultimate goal at which you are currently aiming, then you really should think about reevaluating your goals.

9

The Pilgrim Way and the Christian Philosophical Way of Life

Hidden Assumption No. 4: The Christian Life and Ministry Have Nothing to Do with the Philosophical Life and the Cultivation of the Intellect

We turn in this chapter and the next to examine our fourth and final potential assumption lurking behind practicality questions: that the Christian life and ministry have nothing to do with the philosophical life and the cultivation of the intellect. When someone asks, "How can the study of philosophy possibly be of use to the Christian life, evangelism, and ministry?" I immediately begin to gently inquire what exactly they mean by each of these terms. This well-meant practicality question is often motivated by a view of the Christian life and of ministry that is held hostage by the value assumptions of the workaday world, a view in which intellectual maturity (1 Cor. 14:20; 2 Cor. 10:5) and becoming increasingly attuned to what is real, true, and good are optional leather trim rather than standard operating features of the Christian life and ministry.[1]

I think a more helpful way forward is to fix our eyes and feed our imaginations on a vision of the Christian life, discipleship, and mission that organically arises from the biblical witness itself—one that has been widely employed throughout the Christian tradition.

The Christian Life as the Pilgrim Way

The Christian life is one of pilgrimage from a place of restless spiritual exile to a homecoming of restful communion with God, and we are all somewhere along the way. An interactive and abundant life with the triune God this side of eternity is portrayed throughout Scripture as a journey along a "path of life" (Ps. 16:11) that is "straight" (Prov. 11:5), "level" (Isa. 26:7), "good" (Prov. 2:20), and "ancient" (Jer. 6:16). The book of Acts even describes some of the earliest travelers on this Christ-blazed path as followers of "the Way," which indicates *a way of life* rather than *merely* a body of doctrinal teaching that one mentally affirms (Acts 9:1–2; 19:9, 23; 22:4; 24:14, 22).

Pilgrims on the Way of Christ are to continually "walk" along the path of life in a "manner worthy of the Lord" (Rom. 6:4; Eph. 2:10; 5:15–16; Col. 1:10; 4:5), which means (at least in part) that the everyday lives of wayfarers on this path should bear an increasing resemblance to the full and abundant life of the path's original trailblazer, the triune God as revealed in the person of Christ (Luke 6:40). In fact, "Whoever says he abides in him ought to walk in the

---

1. I again borrow this illustrative concept from Kevin Vanhoozer in Vanhoozer and Strachan, *Pastor as Public Theologian*, 27.

same way in which he walked" (1 John 2:6). In this way, the hearts, minds, and feet of those who sojourn along this path will become increasingly aligned with the true and the good, as indicated by the Christian existential map—filled with abundant and life-giving fruit of the Holy Spirit (Jer. 17:7–8; Eph. 4:1–3) and "increasing in the knowledge of God" (Col. 1:10) and "walking in the truth" (2 John 4; 3 John 4).

Scripture identifies "light" as a defining mark of both the path of Christ and its traveling wayfarers. The idea of light (and darkness) in Scripture is like a complex jewel with many facets. For our purposes here, it is important to emphasize the *moral* and *intellectual* facets of what it means to "walk in the light" along the path of life. Because God himself is light (1 John 1:5), we ought to "walk in the light, as he is in the light" (1:7). As a child seeks to imitate the actions of his or her earthly father, so too "children of light" (Eph. 5:8) are to "be imitators of God, as beloved children" (5:1) for God is "the Father of lights, with whom there is no variation or shadow due to change" (James 1:17).

Scripture weds *light* and *truth* in intriguing ways (Pss. 43:3; 119:105; 2 Cor. 4:4–5; Eph. 5:8–10), so much so that walking in the light amounts to bearing witness to and practicing the truth (1 John 1:7–8; 2:8), while deviating from the path of life toward the "ways of darkness" (Prov. 2:13) amounts to walking in falsehood and illusion (2 Kings 17:15), "futility" of mind, and being "darkened" in understanding (Eph. 4:17–18). Indeed, "The way of the wicked is like deep darkness; they do not know over what they stumble" (Prov. 4:19; see also v. 18). Christians are beckoned to sojourn along the everlastingly good and true way, illumined by God's marvelous light and truth (Ps. 43:3; 1 Pet. 2:9)—a way that is "like the light of dawn, which shines brighter and brighter until full day" (Prov. 4:18; see also v. 19; Rom. 13:12–13). In doing so, we travel a well-worn, ancient road by which we find "rest for [our] souls" (Jer. 6:16).

Immediately after charging Christian pilgrims to "walk as children of light," the apostle Paul says that "the fruit of light is found in all that is *good* and *right* and *true*" (Eph. 5:8–9). Don't miss the gravity of this point: progress in the journey of the Christian life *at its very heart* is evidenced by an increasingly luminous perception of reality and by being rightly oriented to it in all its God-bathed truth, goodness, and beauty. In fact, the apostle John even says that those who deviate from this well-illuminated path walk in darkness and no longer "practice the truth" (1 John 1:6).

The Ultimate End of the Pilgrim Way: The Beatific Vision

If the Christian life is a pilgrimage on the Way, where does the path lead in the end? What is the final end of our earthly striving? What is our existential home and final place of soul rest, we might say? The word "end" can mean two things in this context: either a final resting point (e.g., "the end of the road") or, more classically, a built-in directedness or *telos* toward a particular outcome, what something is *for* by nature (e.g., a pen's end or *telos* is, by nature, directed toward writing and not eating). It turns out that the end of our earthly wayfaring (*end* in the first sense) and the end embedded in human nature itself (*end* in the *telos* sense) are one and the same reality: communion with God in complete knowledge and love.[2]

---

2. The Christian life as a transformative pilgrimage to beatitude has been a rich theme in the history of Christian philosophy, literature, theology, and spirituality. The theme of pilgrimage or journey from exile to beatitude spans the entire Christian tradition (Roman Catholic, Eastern Orthodox, and Protestant) and is beautifully depicted throughout a variety of literary genres, including epic poetry (Dante's *Divine Comedy*), allegory (John Bunyan's *Pilgrim's Progress*, C. S. Lewis's *Pilgrim's Regress*), systematic theology (Anselm of Canterbury's *Proslogion*, Thomas Aquinas's *Summa theologiae*, Bonaventure's *Breviloquium*), and Christian spiritual-devotional writings (Augustine's *On Music*, Teresa of Avila's *Interior Castle*, Bonaventure's *Journey of*

While this full divine-human communion is portrayed in a host of striking and beautiful ways throughout Scripture (e.g., bride/bridegroom), one of the most thought-provoking ways is in terms of the metaphor of *vision* or *sight*. We were created to see and savor God in all his glory, radiance, and goodness. As the only earthly creatures that bear the divine image (Gen. 1:27–28), we were uniquely created with the intellectual and moral capacities to experience such God-directed wonder, to "dwell in the house of the LORD" and "to *gaze* upon the beauty of the LORD and to *inquire* in his temple" (Ps. 27:4); we alone are summoned into the divine presence to behold him and to "taste and see that the LORD is good" (Ps. 34:8), the very purpose for which we were created and redeemed from sin (Exod. 3:12; 29:46).

Since we were tailor-made for God as a key is tailor-made for a lock, only he can truly satisfy us and thus bring our deepest strivings to an end. C. S. Lewis put it so well:

> God made us: invented us as a man invents an engine. A car is made to run on petrol, and it would not run properly on anything else. Now God designed the human machine to run on Himself. He Himself is the fuel our spirits were designed to burn, or the food our spirits were designed to feed on. There is no other. That is why it is just no good asking God to make us happy in our own way without bothering about religion. God cannot give us a happiness and peace apart from Himself, because it is not there.[3]

Scripture also bears witness to a day when we will actually behold God with a fullness and completeness that is consistent with our creaturely finitude. On that day, we will no longer "see in a mirror dimly, but . . . face to face" (1 Cor. 13:12), and "when he appears . . .

---

the *Mind to God*, John of the Cross's *Ascent of Mount Carmel, Dark Night of the Soul*, and *Living Flame of Love*).

3. Lewis, *Mere Christianity*, 50.

we shall see him as he is" (1 John 3:2). The kind of loving closeness to God that awaits those who currently sojourn on the Way is so full and complete, lacking nothing, that it is best described as a "face-to-face" vision of God (see Rev. 22:4).

Historically, this soul-satisfying vision of God (*visio Dei*) that awaits his earthly wayfarers has been called the "beatific vision" because it is the complete and full possession of creaturely beatitude or blessedness (happiness). The beatific vision is the end of the Christian life along the pilgrim way as well as the ultimate end (*telos*) of human existence. When we see God in this way, we will experience an even greater measure of his incomparable vastness and will be continually transformed to take more of him in as we do; the experience of complete, soul-satisfying wonder is our awaited portion and ultimate *telos*.[4] As theologian Hans Boersma puts it in his excellent book-length treatment on the beatific vision, "For all traditional forms of Christianity the 'beatific vision,' gazing on God in utmost joy, is the ultimate goal of Christian living, the fulfillment of our Christian discipleship."[5]

As creaturely wayfarers that are "bound for beatitude,"[6] our present vision of God's radiant truth and goodness will be partial as we "see in a mirror dimly" and "walk by faith, not by sight" (1 Cor. 13:12; 2 Cor. 5:6–7). The illuminating nature of Scripture serves as the triune God's ever-shining light by which he instructs and guides his wayfaring pilgrims on the journey home. Amid "a crooked and twisted generation," Scripture is a lamp and a light for travelers on

---

4. Augustine begins and ends his *Confessions* (see 1.1 and 13.35–38, pp. 3 and 304) with the theme of soul rest, using a literary device known as *inclusio* (bookending a literary work with a particular theme or emphasis). The restless heart strives for rest and peace here on earth, bouncing from creature to creature, until it lays hold of its true object, God, partially now and fully in the beatific vision to come.

5. Boersma, *Seeing God*, xiii.

6. I borrow this phrase from the title of Reinhard Hutter's book *Bound for Beatitude: A Thomistic Study in Eschatology and Ethics*.

the Way who seek to "shine as lights in the world, holding fast to the word of life" (Phil. 2:15–16; see also Ps. 119:105).

Yet, because of the weight of sin that clings so closely to our feet and distorts our view of the path of life, we catch satisfying but only momentary glimpses of the triune God in the face of Christ. This is precisely why those currently on the Way to beatitude are called to "strive for . . . the holiness without which no one will see the Lord" (Heb. 12:14; see also Matt. 5:8). The degree to which we are able to see God in the face of Christ *now* depends on the degree to which our hearts and minds are being cleansed and purified by divine grace.

All our creaturely powers are summoned to this, our greatest earthly task, since "this contemplation is promised to us as the end of all our labors and the eternal fullness of our joys."[7] We are charged to strain forward and "press on toward the goal for the prize of the upward call of God in Christ Jesus" (Phil. 3:13–14), to lay aside our sin and see and savor God in Christ until that day when our dim faith will be transformed into luminous sight. Yet, until that day, our hearts will continue to yearn to attain full communion with the One for whom we were made and will remain restless to some degree or other until they attain it. Yet, by God's mysterious grace and empowering Spirit, a foretaste of the beatific vision is available *now* to wayfarers whose hearts and minds are single-mindedly devoted to "beholding the glory of the Lord" and "are being transformed into the same image from one degree of glory to another" (2 Cor. 3:18).

Living Philosophically along the Way

So we've seen that Scripture paints a vivid picture of the Christian life and ministry as one of pilgrimage whose end is the beatific vision of

---

7. Augustine, *Trinity* 1.8, pp. 23–24.

God in the life to come. But how exactly does this conception of the Christian life and ministry bear on the final hidden assumption lurking behind practicality questions: that the Christian life and ministry have nothing to do with the philosophical life and the cultivation of the intellect?

My aim here and in chapter 10 will be, with the help of a few of my much older and wiser (and now dead) friends, to provide three ways to connect the dots regarding how living philosophically as a Christian can help us make progress along the Way to beatitude (and help us come to the aid of fellow wayfarers):

- by empowering us to live out of an active intellectual posture toward weighty and life-altering ideas along the Way
- by administering mind's-eye therapeutics along the Way
- by making us fit to enjoy earthly foretastes of heavenly beatitude along the Way

I will take up the first two points in the rest of this chapter and then turn to the third point in chapter 10.

Christian Philosophy and Two Intellectual Postures along the Way

One way in which the Christian philosophical way of life can deepen the Christian life and empower our mission in the world is by helping us cultivate an active, truth-oriented, and evidence-sensitive posture toward weighty and life-altering ideas. According to the apostle Paul, there are two basic postures one can adopt regarding ideas in particular and the intellectual life in general—an *active* posture or a *passive* posture. We will inevitably adopt either one or the other; there is no middle ground.

Babes in Christ, those of small spiritual stature, are largely *passive* when it comes to soul-destructive ideas that are contrary to the gospel; they are taken captive (Col. 2:8) and "tossed to and fro" and "carried about by every wind of doctrine" (Eph. 4:14). Like a toy rubber duck hurled headlong into the turbulent waves of the sea, the spiritually immature person lacks intellectual stability and is thus all the more susceptible to the glittering allure of rival visions of the true, good, and beautiful.

For the apostle Paul, "to grow up in every way" into Christ (Eph. 4:15) clearly involves outgrowing this idle intellectual posture and embracing a more *active*, engaged, and sure-footed posture regarding the intellectual life. Paul admonishes, "Do not be children in your thinking. Be infants in evil, but in your thinking be mature" (1 Cor. 14:20). This active posture is stated clearly in 2 Corinthians 10:5: "We destroy arguments and every lofty opinion raised against the knowledge of God, and take every thought captive to obey Christ." Stable, mature Christians display a readiness to "take every thought captive" and have the ability to ensure that they are not taken "captive by philosophy and empty deceit, according to human tradition . . . and not according to Christ" (Col. 2:8). Sure-footed and seasoned travelers of the Way are called to be *captors* of false and life-denying ideas (an active posture), not *captives* of them (a passive posture).

Paul's emphasis on an active intellectual posture and the importance of intellectual growth and stability in the life of the Christian is on full display in his own ministry, recorded for us in the book of Acts. Throughout Acts, we find Paul regularly devoting himself to ministry oriented around the engagement with and refutation of false and destructive ideas. In Acts 17, we find Paul engaging the intellectual elite in Athens by quoting pagan sources from memory (v. 28) as well as ministering to the Jews in Thessalonica even as he "reasoned with them from the Scriptures, explaining and proving that it was necessary for the Christ to suffer and to rise from the dead" (vv. 2–3).

Luke even points out that some were persuaded and decided to follow Paul and Silas as a result of his public, truth-oriented intellectual endeavors in Thessalonica (v. 4). In fact, Luke sees fit to emphasize that Paul's intellectual engagement was a *regular* and *customary* part of the apostle's ministry (v. 2): it was not a mere one-off moment but an enduring *way of life*.

In fact, in Acts 19:8–10, Luke tells us that in Ephesus Paul "entered the synagogue and for three months spoke boldly, reasoning and persuading them [the Jews] about the kingdom of God." After his efforts were met with fierce opposition and resistance, Paul "withdrew from them and took the disciples with him, reasoning daily in the hall of Tyrannus." Luke goes on to say that Paul's daily, active intellectual labors in the hall of Tyrannus, a local lecture hall, lasted two full years. What was the impact of Paul's fervent commitment to a two-year period of robust intellectual discipleship and outreach in Ephesus? We do not have to speculate, because Luke tells us in the very next verse that "all the residents of Asia heard the word of the Lord, both Jews and Greeks" (v. 10). Strategic and active intellectual engagement can yield significant impact for the kingdom.

While Christian discipleship and ministry involves much more than taking up this active posture in the intellectual life, it most certainly involves nothing less. And living philosophically as a Christian is one important way that Christian pilgrims can cultivate this active intellectual posture along the Way.

Christian Philosophy as Mind's-Eye Therapeutics along the Way

Many of us currently on the Way are painfully aware of the heaviness of our sin and the ways that it binds our feet, clouds our heavenly vision, and thus pulls our gaze downward toward "worthless things" (Ps. 119:37). We deeply resonate with the Italian poet and Christian thinker Dante Alighieri (1265–1321) and his apt description, at the beginning of his poetic masterpiece *The Divine Comedy*, of our creaturely waywardness this side of the beatific vision: "Midway upon the journey of our life I found myself in a dark wilderness, for I had wandered from the straight and true."[8] Though we long, by nature, to walk the straight and true path of life, we nevertheless are prone to wander and often prefer various "shadows of happiness" to the true substance of our highest good, God.[9] The human heart seeks the good and straight path of life and true happiness, yet "like a drunkard it cannot find the path home."[10] As Lady Philosophy helpfully reminds us, these false visions of reality and the good life are "sidetracks and cannot bring us to the destination they promise."[11]

Given our natures and their embedded, goal-directed ends, our most pressing earthly need here and now is to clearly see and steadily walk along the path of life in Christ and not deviate from it, and to help others do the same. And the greatest thing we can do for other people this side of eternity, whether Christians or non-Christians, is to shine light on the insufficiency of dimly lit and wayward "sidetracks" and help them clearly see and lay hold of the One who is "the way, and the truth, and the life" (John 14:6). Only then can we be properly attuned to and fully at home in God's reality, "for the glory of God is a living man; and the life of man consists in beholding God."[12]

Our proneness to wander down the various sidetracks of life and our ever-increasing loss of vision of the true and the good has two possible causes. On the one hand, our waywardness may be the

---

8. Dante, *Inferno* 1.1–3.
9. Boethius, *Consolation of Philosophy* 3.1, p. 47.
10. Boethius, *Consolation of Philosophy* 3.2, p. 49.
11. Boethius, *Consolation of Philosophy* 3.8, p. 60.
12. "Irenaeus against Heresies," in Irenaeus, *Apostolic Fathers with Justin Martyr and Irenaeus*, 490.

result of our own inherited tendency to prefer a path of our own making, one blazed on our own terms: what Scripture often refers to as walking "according to the flesh" (Rom. 8:5). Those who choose to walk entirely on a path of their own making "set their minds on the things of the flesh" (Rom. 8:5) and thus inevitably twist and misdirect their intellectual and moral powers toward unfitting ends.[13] And the consequences couldn't be more devastating to human life, because this misdirection naturally leads to "the futility of their minds" and causes them to be "darkened in their understanding" and thus tragically "alienated from the life of God" (Eph. 4:17–19; cf. Heb. 3:12–13). And the one who wanders in the darkness, as the apostle John reminds us, "does not know where he is going, because the darkness has blinded his eyes" (1 John 2:11). Alienation and perpetual exile from our true home, from the life of the triune God himself, is the natural consequence of sojourning on a darkened path of our own making.

On the other hand, we must also take very seriously the fact that our creaturely waywardness on the road to beatitude may alternatively—or additionally—be the result of sinister spiritual powers who are actively and methodically working to flood our mind's eye with darkness instead of light and to lure us from the Way by the deceitful pleasures of sin (Eph. 4:14; 6:11). The "god of this world" seeks to divert our gaze from a clear-eyed vision of the true and the good in Christ (2 Cor. 4:4).

Whatever the cause of our creaturely waywardness, we are all in dire need of a mind's-eye physician, someone who can properly diagnose and administer therapeutic remedies for our loss of sight and proneness to prefer paths of our own making. As Augustine put it, "What is it

---

13. For discussion of the idea of a morally disordered intellectual life, see "Curiosity," in Webster, *Domain of the Word*, 193–202. See also Inman, "Epistemic Temperance."

that inflames the eyes of the heart? Greed, avarice, injustice, worldly covetousness inflames, closes, blinds the eye of the heart. And yet how they go looking for a doctor when the eye of the body gets inflamed, how they rush without delay to get it opened and cleaned out, to restore the capacity to see this light!" Augustine's point is that if we don't hesitate to seek medical attention when our physical eyes are inflamed and swollen shut, how much *more* should we seek the proper therapeutics when the eyes of our soul are hindered from seeing the source and stability of our true good, the triune God himself? Augustine is right, then, when he says, "What calls for all our efforts *in this life* is the healing of the eyes of our hearts, with which God is to be seen."[14]

In this way, living philosophically as a Christian can serve as restorative first aid to one whose mind's eye is weak and failing, unable to properly see God and abide in the Way of Christ. One of the most detailed examples of this restorative and therapeutic function of Christian philosophy along the Way comes from the Christian thinker Hugh of Saint Victor (1096–1141) in his work *Didascalicon on the Study of Reading*. For Hugh, sin clouds the mind and weakens the will, resulting in the mind being "numbed by bodily passions" and the divine likeness in us being tarnished and in need of restoration. The divine likeness that once shone brightly in us "must be restored by training" and "regulated by applying a remedy."[15] This restorative training or remedy consists "first in the philosophical disciplines then in Sacred Scripture, that the human person participates in and facilitates divine Wisdom's work of re-ordering him toward self-knowledge and, ultimately, knowledge and love of God."[16]

According to Hugh, "there are two things that restore the divine likeness in the human person, namely, the investigation of truth and

---

14. "Sermon 88.6," in Augustine, *Sermons 51–94*, 422–23 (emphasis added).
15. Hugh, *Didascalicon* 1.5, p. 88.
16. Harkins, "Introduction to *Didascalicon*," 66.

the practice of virtue."[17] Drawing on older, classical thinkers such as Boethius, Hugh defines philosophy very broadly as "the discipline that plausibly investigates the reasons of all things, both divine and human," and as "the love and pursuit of, and in a certain way friendship with, Wisdom" (which he identifies ultimately with Christ). For Hugh, philosophical study in this broad sense encompasses what he calls the *theoretical arts* or the quadrivium, such as theology, arithmetic, music, geometry, and astronomy (aimed at rightly ordering the mind toward the true); the *practical arts*, such as ethics, economics, and politics (aimed at rightly ordering the will toward the good); the *mechanical arts*, such as commerce, agriculture, hunting, medicine, and theater (aimed at rightly ordering human affairs); and the *logical arts* or the trivium, such as grammar, rhetoric, and logic/dialectic (aimed at rightly ordering human thinking).[18]

Because the theoretical and practical aspects of philosophy are aimed at the investigation of the true and alignment with the good, they help heal our dullness of sight and ingrown wills. They are instruments to prepare a way (*via*) "for the mind to arrive at full knowledge of philosophical truth" and "certain roads by which the vigorous mind enters into the hidden places of wisdom."[19] Hugh draws from this a striking conclusion: "The greatest solace in life, therefore, is the pursuit of Wisdom."[20]

By following in Hugh's footsteps and by committing to an existential map shaped by the Christian story and structuring one's everyday life around it (including the regular practice of soul *askesis*), practitioners of a Christian philosophical way of life submit to regular mind's-eye exams. They do so by striving to live in tune with the real, the true, and the good (with the grain of reality) and by the

17. Hugh, *Didascalicon* 1.7, p. 90.
18. Hugh, *Didascalicon* 2.1, pp. 96–97.
19. Hugh, *Didascalicon* 3.3, p. 120.
20. Hugh, *Didascalicon* 1.1, p. 84.

regular practice of the truth-oriented spiritual exercises of silence, solitude, meditation, and self-examination, along with an openness to the course-corrective and stabilizing influence of spiritual friends. They recognize that progress on the Way (including helping others to find it and stably walk in it) crucially depends on being the kind of person who is properly aligned with the grain of reality.

Indeed, according to Augustine, restoring the health of the mind and heart for the purpose of seeing God more clearly is the very way in which we progress on the journey to beatitude. He says that "the soul must be purified that it may have power to perceive that light, and to rest in it when it is perceived. *And let us look upon this purification as a kind of journey or voyage to our native land.* For it is not by change of place that we can come nearer to Him who is in every place, but by the cultivation of pure desires and virtuous habits."[21]

The Christian philosophical way of life, as a truth-directed and spiritually transformative way of walking the road to beatitude, can help restore the dull and diverted mind to what is true and orient the will to what is good here and now.

21. "On Christian Doctrine," in *St. Augustine's City of God and Christian Doctrine*, 525 (emphasis added).

10

Philosophy, the Contemplative Life, and the Church

Thus far we've seen that both Scripture and the Christian tradition bear witness that the depth and shape of one's intellectual life is a vitally important aspect of Christian formation and ministry. This stands in direct tension with the last hidden assumption lurking behind practicality questions: that the Christian life and ministry have nothing to do with the philosophical life and the cultivation of the intellect. And, once again, the reason is that the subjects of Christian discipleship and formation are *human persons*. The formation of human persons in Christ ought to strengthen and deepen every facet of the human person, including the intellect, "until Christ is formed" in them (Gal. 4:19). Maturing in Christ involves (at least in part) cultivating a more capacious mind that is increasingly fit to lovingly behold its highest object, God himself, and to walk wisely along the natural grain of reality that God has laid down in creation.

To neglect this crucial aspect of Christian formation is to neglect *human* formation.

Scripture routinely reminds us of the importance of becoming more mindful of morally and spiritually weighty matters as we sojourn on the Way to beatitude (Matt. 6:19–24; 2 Cor. 3:18; 4:16–18; Phil. 4:8; Col. 3:1–2).[1] Yet, as I noted in chapter 7, while you've likely heard it said (or may have said yourself!) that we shouldn't be so heavenly minded as to be of no earthly good, there is a flip side to this cautionary word: at the end of the day, I think it misses the vital importance that Scripture places on cultivating a greater heavenly attention as *the very means by which* we experience a foretaste of beatitude here and now.

Rather, we should be *so heavenly minded that we are of some earthly good.* If our mind's eye remains exclusively fixed on inferior loves and pursuits, we will never be able to be truly "rich toward God" and lay hold of "that which is truly life" (Luke 12:13–21; 1 Tim. 6:19), let alone help others do the same. In his book *Mere Christianity*, C. S. Lewis puts this point in a characteristically clear light:

> A continual looking forward to the eternal world is not (as some modern people think) a form of escapism or wishful thinking, but one of the things a Christian is meant to do. It does not mean that we are to leave the present world as it is. If you read history you will find that the Christians who did most for the present world were just those who thought most of the next. The Apostles themselves, who set on foot the conversion of the Roman Empire, the great men who built up the Middle Ages, the English Evangelicals who abolished the Slave Trade, all left their mark on Earth, precisely because their minds were occupied with Heaven. It is since Christians have largely ceased to think of the other world that they have become so ineffective in this. Aim at Heaven and you will get earth "thrown in": aim at earth and you will get neither.[2]

1. I recommend that readers pause here and carefully ponder each of these texts.
2. Lewis, *Mere Christianity*, 135.

Along the same lines, Hebrews 11:13–16, summarizing those who belong to the "great . . . cloud of witnesses" (12:1) who left a sizable imprint for God and his kingdom while on earth, makes the point that these individuals were able to make such a deep earthly footprint precisely *because* they were "seeking a homeland" (11:14) and longed for "a better country, that is, a heavenly one" (v. 16) as they walked the good and ancient path (Jer. 6:16). Theologian Michael Allen drives this point home when he says, "Heavenly-mindedness is part of the very warp and woof of Christian discipleship, not some mere appendage."[3]

Contemplation as a Foretaste of Beatitude along the Way

In the wider Christian tradition, the task of cultivating deep attention to morally and spiritually weighty matters has traditionally been called *contemplation*. Contemplation and its role in Christian formation along the Way is multifaceted and complex and much too broad for me to fully unpack here. But I'm convinced that contemplation is, at bottom, an essential conduit by which our natural appetite for wonder—our hunger to be moved by and to make sense of it all—is ultimately satisfied. We were created to lovingly behold the vastness of the triune God and the natural grain that is the work of his wise hands and to humbly fit our small selves into his all-expansive life that sustains all things in love.[4]

My limited purpose in this final chapter is to introduce you to two of my older and much wiser medieval friends, Anselm of Canterbury

3. M. Allen, *Grounded in Heaven*, 90.
4. For a medieval Christian writer who explicitly links contemplation with wonder, see Richard of St. Victor, *Mystical Ark*, esp. chap. 4. Richard says, "Contemplation is the free, more penetrating gaze of the mind, suspended with wonder concerning manifestations of wisdom," and "it is the property of contemplation to cling with wonder to the manifestation of its joy" (157).

and Thomas Aquinas, who can help us find clarity about how the Christian philosophical way of life bears on the contemplative life. These two sure-footed guides can shed light on how contemplation within the community of saints can aid in furthering the end of the Christian life by cultivating a greater foretaste of beatitude along the Way and helping others do the same.

Anselm of Canterbury: From Our Homeland into Exile, and Back Again via Contemplation

One of the most notable examples of how contemplation and the Christian philosophical way of life can be explicitly situated within our journey to beatitude is provided by the Christian thinker Anselm of Canterbury (1033–1109). Anselm was a brilliant theologian, philosopher, and reluctant administrator who would later become the archbishop of Canterbury. He spent most of his adult life ministering to his fellow Benedictine monks and leading them in Christian contemplation and meditative exercises on the great truths of the Christian faith.

According to Anselm, we are uniquely created in God's image with the creaturely capacities to see and savor God in a communion of everlasting love. Anselm believed that God himself is our final end and supreme good, the only one who can bring the soul true rest and lasting joy: "Human beings, who are rational in nature, were made just in order that they might be happy in enjoying God."[5]

Yet Anselm was convinced, following the lead of his intellectual forefather Augustine, that *we cannot love what we do not know.*[6] To put it differently, the degree to which we can *love* and *delight* in another is directly related to the degree to which we *know* the other.

---

5. *Cur Deus homo* 2.1, in *Anselm: Basic Writings*, 290.
6. Augustine, *Trinity* 10.1, p. 291.

From this principle, together with the truth that we were created to love and enjoy God as our supreme good and final end, Anselm makes a striking conclusion about the operation of our intellectual powers in the pursuit of God *here and now*: "It is therefore clear that the rational creature ought to devote all its power and will to remembering and understanding and loving the supreme good, for which purpose it knows it has its very existence."[7] According to Anselm, it is our native posture in life to strain with all our creaturely might, with every facet of our being (intellect and will), to clearly see and orient our lives to the One who is our final end and beatitude. It's what we were made for.

Despite being the kinds of creatures who, by nature, have an appetite for the love and enjoyment of God, the tragic reality is that our first human parents, Adam and Eve, willfully turned inward and cut themselves off from God as their greatest good and "fountain of life" (Ps. 36:9). Sin has subsequently distorted and blinded the very intellectual capacities God has given us to clearly see him and thereby love him and enjoy him. As a result, all children of Adam and Eve "have lost the happiness for which they were created and found an unhappiness for which they were not created."[8] We have been driven "from our homeland into exile; from the vision of God into our blindness; from the joy of immortality into the bitterness and terror of death." Anselm says, "I acknowledge, Lord, and I thank you, that you have created in me this image of you so that I may remember you, think of you, and love you. Yet this image is so eroded by my vices, so clouded by the smoke of my sins, that it cannot do what it was created to do unless you renew and refashion it."[9]

For Anselm, the prospects of our being freed from exile and guided back to our God-ordained homeland—the vision of God—are

---

7. *Monologion 68*, in *Anselm: Basic Writings*, 66.
8. *Proslogion 1*, in *Anselm: Basic Writings*, 79.
9. *Proslogion 1*, in *Anselm: Basic Writings*, 81.

completely hopeless if we are left to ourselves. But since God in his bountiful goodness has "a mysterious bias towards mercy,"[10] we are not left to ourselves. God graciously takes the initiative and begins the process of "renewing and refashioning" our creaturely intellect and will to make us fit once again for the journey back home to the vision of God. And this is exactly what Anselm pleads that God would continually do: "Cleanse, heal, sharpen, 'enlighten the eye' of my soul so that I may look upon you. Let my soul gather its strength, and let it once more strive with all its understanding to reach you, O Lord."[11] The intellectual and moral capacities of wayfaring creatures like us have been created and redeemed and are being continually renewed for the journey onward and upward to our heavenly homeland.

Anselm is a notable expression of one particular way to live philosophically as a Christian: he went on to use his grace-renewed intellectual powers to create some of the richest and most enduring philosophical, theological, and spiritual writings in the Christian tradition. He employed every facet of his God-given nature for the purpose of contemplating (and helping others to contemplate) spiritually weighty matters such as the existence and nature of God, the Trinity, creation, the person of Christ and his saving work, and the natures of free will and truth.

Thomas Aquinas: Contemplation as Tasting and Seeing Heaven Here on Earth

We now turn to Thomas Aquinas (1225–1274), the great medieval Christian theologian, philosopher, and scriptural commentator. Aquinas defined contemplation in its broadest sense as "nothing else

10. Adams, "*Fides quaerens intellectum*," 410.
11. *Proslogion* 18, in *Anselm: Basic Writings*, 91.

than the consideration of truth, which is the good of the intellect."[12] For Aquinas, our intellect has a natural, God-given appetite for truth and is satisfied only when it feeds upon truth, we might say. As an intellectual activity that fulfills one of our natural, God-given capacities, contemplation in this broad sense is intrinsically valuable and is an essential ingredient of our flourishing *as humans*; contemplation "is ordered to nothing else as an end, for the contemplation of truth is sought for its own sake."[13]

More specifically, Aquinas distinguishes between what he calls "perfect" and "imperfect" contemplation as two kinds of consideration of truth.[14] Perfect contemplation is the kind of consideration of truth that awaits all sojourners on the Way of Christ in the life to come and is the source of what Aquinas calls "perfect happiness";[15] perfect contemplation is full and immediate and is a kind of intuitive vision of the triune God.[16] Since in the life to come we will be wholly without sin and moral defect, perfect contemplation is the fitting mode by which we are united to the triune God as citizens of our heavenly home: "the Fatherland," as Aquinas calls it.

Imperfect contemplation, by contrast, is the consideration of truth that is partial, mediated through creatures, and is the source of "imperfect happiness." Aquinas's notion of imperfect contemplation is referred to as "earthly contemplation" by some, since he believes it pertains to our consideration of truth on the road to

---

12. Thomas Aquinas, *Summa theologiae* I-II, q. 35, art. 5, ad. 3, p. 691.

13. Thomas Aquinas, *Summa contra Gentiles* 3.37.3, p. 124.

14. *Commentary on the Sentences*, q. 1, art. 1, in *Thomas Aquinas: Selected Writings*, 56. See also Thomas Aquinas, *Summa theologiae* II-II, q. 180, art. 7, ad. 1, p. 702.

15. Thomas Aquinas, *Summa theologiae* I-II, q. 3, art. 2, pp. 31–32.

16. By "intuitive vision" I mean something like an all-at-once beholding of what we can take in of the triune God as finite creatures—a beholding that engages every facet of the human rather than a piece-by-piece beholding that proceeds by a step-by-step chain of reasoning and leads to a conclusion.

beatitude *here and now*.[17] Aquinas construes earthly or incomplete contemplation arguably broad enough to include the consideration of truth here and now both from the standpoint and foundation of divine revelation (sacred doctrine or theology) and from the standpoint and foundation of human reason (philosophy).[18] Because he explicitly appeals to Aristotle's notion of philosophical contemplation (outlined in book 10 of Aristotle's *Nicomachean Ethics*) in this context as a "happiness 'on the way,' of this life,"[19] Aquinas clearly means to include philosophical contemplation as a form of earthly contemplation and thus an ingredient of the imperfect happiness available to us here and now.

For Aquinas, earthly contemplation is an intellectual exercise that is propelled by love and brings, in turn, deeper love, delight, and joy in its wake.[20] As we will see in more detail below, earthly contemplation—in both its philosophical and its theological forms—can put before us satisfying albeit partial tastes of the heavenly beatitude that is our full portion to come; it is "the ladder that leads up to the beatific vision."[21] Yet the ability to enjoy earthly contemplation is not at our disposal at the simple snap of our fingers, irrespective of the kind of persons we are. Rather, the moral and intellectual virtues that are cultivated by way of Christian spiritual exercises (*askesis*) help *prepare* or *dispose* us for the earthly contemplative life; they make us the *kinds of persons* who are more apt to catch clearer and

17. See "Earthly Contemplation," in *Josef Pieper: An Anthology*, 143–48; and Van Nieuwenhove, *Thomas Aquinas and Contemplation*. See also Thomas Aquinas, *Summa contra Gentiles* 3.63, p. 209.

18. For the argument that Aquinas includes both theological and philosophical contemplation under "incomplete contemplation" (and not just philosophical contemplation), see Van Nieuwenhove, *Thomas Aquinas and Contemplation*, chap. 1.

19. *Commentary on the Sentences*, q. 1, art.1, in *Thomas Aquinas: Selected Writings*, 56.

20. Thomas Aquinas, *Summa theologiae* II-II, q. 180, art. 7, ad. 1, p. 702.

21. Pieper, *Philosophical Act*, 114.

more satisfying glimpses of the true depth of created reality as well as of our highest good, God himself.

It is important to point out that, for Aquinas, the two earthly forms of contemplation on the road to beatitude—theological and philosophical contemplation—should not be thought of as two separate roads. Rather, they are two distinct, complementary *ways* of traveling one and the same road to the vision of God in the life to come. They are, to use another apt metaphor, "like two wings on which the human spirit rises to the contemplation of truth."[22] While earthly theological contemplation is more excellent and delightful for wayfarers on account of the supreme truth, goodness, and beauty of the One contemplated, the consideration of truth by means of earthly philosophical contemplation also serves to satisfy our natural appetite to feed upon truth.

Along these lines, Christian theologian Frederick Bauerschmidt masterfully explains Aquinas's general view of the relationship between reason and Christian faith: "Though guided by both the pillar of cloud and the pillar of fire, the journey of the Israelites is only one journey, and it is a journey toward the promised gift of beatitude. Though Thomas employs both natural human reason and supernaturally infused faith, it is all part of the one way of life of holy teaching."[23] Since the *Christian* philosophical way of life (including the practice of earthly contemplation) will always be ultimately rooted and anchored in the Christian story and its various existential coordinates, it will never be *exclusively* philosophical but will proceed from a robust theological vision of God and of all things in relation to God.

How might Aquinas's notion of earthly philosophical contemplation bear on the Christian life and ministry for pilgrims on the Way?

22. John Paul II, "Fides et ratio."
23. Bauerschmidt, *Thomas Aquinas*, 76.

What role might earthly contemplation play in ministering to fellow sojourners on the Way? After all, by the standards of value of the workaday world, it is difficult if not impossible to discern the measurable results or deliverables of earthly contemplation, especially philosophical contemplation. Yet, according to Aquinas, the contemplative life is vital for making progress along the Way to heavenly beatitude; it is a sanctifying and transformative way of bringing our creaturely intellects and wills into greater alignment with the One who is supreme truth, goodness, and beauty.

In this way, earthy contemplation, in all its forms, *orients* us to and *prepares* us for perfect contemplation, the full and complete beatific vision to come: "There is nothing in this life so like this ultimate and perfect felicity as the life of those who contemplate truth, to the extent that it is possible in this life. . . . In fact, the contemplation of truth begins in this life but reaches its climax in the future."[24] Don't miss the striking claims that Aquinas is putting before us in this passage. For Aquinas, you would look in vain for a brighter earthly reflection of the glory that awaits us in the beatific vision than the life devoted to the contemplation of truth here and now. Even more, our earthly contemplation is the initial seed that is nourished, sprouts, and begins to blossom in the form of a flourishing and wise human life lived along the grain of reality, one that eventually reaches full bloom in the complete, loving contemplation of God in the life to come.

Along these same lines, Aquinas emphasizes the incomparable worth and formative role of the pursuit of wisdom for wayfarers on the Way, saying that "among all human pursuits, the pursuit of wisdom is more perfect, more noble, more useful, and more full of joy," since by it we come to "have some share in true beatitude"

---

24. Thomas Aquinas, *Summa contra Gentiles* 3.63, p. 209, quoted in Van Nieuwenhove, *Thomas Aquinas and Contemplation*, 15.

and a greater "likeness to God" here and now.[25] As you can see, we've left the excessively narrow standards of value and worth operative in the workaday world far behind in the rearview mirror. All forms of earthly contemplation and pursuits of wisdom help us wayfarers "grow in conformity and likeness with God."[26] The more we orient our lives here and now around the pursuit of wisdom by means of earthly contemplation in all its theological and philosophical forms, enabled by the ongoing ministry of the Holy Spirit, the more we partake of the beatitude to come and bear a greater family resemblance to God as his beloved children. And if growing in likeness to God and being transformed into the image of his radiant Son (Rom. 12:2; 2 Cor. 3:12–18; Heb. 1:3; 2 Pet. 1:3–15) are not important for Christian discipleship and ministry, I honestly don't know what is.

Yet we should not think Aquinas believes that the Christian calling to the contemplative life is reserved for only a select few (the scholars, theologians, or lowly philosophers, but not the welders). As Christian theologian Rik Van Nieuwenhove has insightfully pointed out, in its widest sense, Aquinas's understanding of contemplation is within the reach of all who strive to employ their God-given creaturely intellectual powers in the task of knowing God and all things in relation to God. The fact that Aquinas roots the call to the earthly contemplative life in the wider command to keep the Sabbath, as well as his view that the virgin Mary excelled in earthly contemplation, reveals that he understood earthly contemplation to be very broad and much more inclusive than Aristotle's idea of philosophical contemplation (*theoria*) as the *theoretical* consideration of truth here and now. Indeed, Aquinas says that "every Christian who is in a state of salvation must participate somehow in contemplation, for

---

25. Thomas Aquinas, *Summa contra Gentiles* 1.2, p. 61.
26. Van Nieuwenhove, *Thomas Aquinas and Contemplation*, 16.

the commandment is given to all: 'Be still and see that I am God'"
(Ps. 46:10).[27]

Nor should we think that the contemplative life, understood in
this sense, is at odds with the outward action-oriented life devoted
to the love and service of others. We've already seen in previous
chapters the inseparable relation between ideas and action: where
the mind goes, so go one's actions. Practitioners of the Christian
philosophical way of life, including those who pursue a life of earthly
philosophical contemplation, are committed to an existential map
of reality and the good life shaped by the Christian story *in addition to* ordering and structuring their lives in light of it. As *a way of
life*, living philosophically as a Christian is thus a way of ordering
the moments of one's everyday life in light of the Christian story,
not merely a mental nod to a cohesive body of doctrine or beliefs.
So the Christian philosophical way of life, *as a way of life*, includes
the action-oriented life.

In this way, then, the contemplative life and the active life feed on
and into each other. As Gregory Nazianzen puts it, "All philosophy is
divided into two aspects, contemplation and practice, . . . [and] each
is seen as valuable because of the other. For we make contemplation
our companion on the way to the next life, and [we make] practice
our means of access to contemplation; after all, it is impossible to
share in wisdom without behaving wisely."[28] With Gregory, Anselm,
and Aquinas, then, we should wed and not rend asunder the life of
contemplation (in all its forms) and the life of Christian mission and
action along the Way.

---

27. *Commentary on the Sentences*, q. 1, art. 3, as quoted in Van Nieuwenhove,
Thomas Aquinas and Contemplation, 4.
28. Gregory Nazianzen, *Oration* 4.113, as quoted in Daley, *Gregory of Nazianzus*, 35.

The Church as Pillar and Cradle of a Christian Philosophical Way of Life

Up to this point, you might have gotten the impression that the Chris
tian pilgrimage along the Way to our heavenly home is one that we
travel on our own. Yet nothing could be further from the truth. I
already noted in chapter 6 the nature and indispensability of *communal* spiritual exercises for the Christian philosophical way of life,
in particular the practice of spiritual friendship. It takes a village, as
they say, to live philosophically as a Christian. In this section we will
consider the nature and role of the church, the corporate people of
God, and how it is indispensable to the Christian philosophical way
of life. We will see that the nature and *telos* of the church in God's
economy is, among other things, to nurture a people who enduringly
abide in, are *stabilized* by, and *herald* the true and the good in Christ.

Corporately, the church of the living God is to embody and uphold
the truth, goodness, and beauty of the gospel of Jesus Christ; it is to
be a pillar of intellectual stability. Paul tells Timothy that the church
of the living God is the "pillar and buttress of the truth" (1 Tim.
3:15). "Buttress" is an architectural word and conveys a source of
defense or reinforcement (try googling "architectural buttress" if you
aren't familiar with the word). It is part of the very nature and function of the corporate people of God to "practice the truth" (1 John
1:6)—that is, to reinforce, defend, and *be the living embodiment of*
the truth of the gospel of Christ.

We should pause here and recognize that this is a point about the
nature of the church, the God-ordained *essence* of the church—what
the church is in its core identity. The church is the type of social collective that is, *by nature*, oriented toward a certain range of ends.
This is different from the question of whether the church is in fact
successful in carrying out the specific embedded ends that belong to it
by nature. We can put it like this: just as an iPhone cannot successfully

develop a healthy root system (it's just not the right *kind* of thing), neither can the church successfully carry out ends that are not, in fact, embedded in it by nature.

So *which* particular ends belong to the church by nature, we might ask? According to the apostle Paul in 1 Timothy 3:15, one specific end to which the church is essentially directed is to be anchored in and bear witness to what truly *is*; the church of the living God is essentially *truth-oriented* by nature. It is important to point out that not all social collectives are oriented by nature to the preservation and defense of what truly is. When I gather with a few friends for a meal or for a run, our gathering is not the sort of gathering that is naturally aimed at the preservation and support of the truth about the totality of things and how it all meaningfully fits together. While we may get into some interesting philosophical conversations while we eat or run (actually, you can count on it!), this is different from saying that the essence or nature of our gathering—what makes our gathering the very gathering it is—is centered on the proclamation and defense of what truly is.

Let this Pauline vision of the nature of Christ's bride sink in a bit. If you were to poll a large group of non-Christians and ask them how they perceive the church of the living God today, would you expect to them to rattle off things like "pillar and buttress of the truth," "cradle of intellectually stability," and so on? Not a chance. What would they say? Thankfully, we don't have to speculate because such statistical research has already been done for us.

In the book *UnChristian*, the Barna Group, an evangelical polling organization, unpacks the findings of a research project that surveyed non-Christians aged 16–29 about their perceived image of the church. One such public perception was that Christians, evangelicals in particular, are "boring, unintelligent, old-fashioned, and out of touch with reality." The Barna Group summarizes this result as follows:

Many outsiders believe Christianity insulates people from thinking. Often young people (including many insiders) doubt that Christianity boosts intellect. We discovered a range of opinions on this, but Christianity is not generally perceived to sanction a thoughtful response to the world. One comment illustrates this image: "Christianity stifles curiosity. People become unwilling to face their doubts and questions. It makes people brain-dead." The vast majority of outsiders reject the idea that Christianity "makes sense" or is "relevant to their life." So part of the sheltered perception is that Christians are not thinkers.[29]

Insulated from thinking, not offering a thoughtful response to the world, stifling curiosity, unwilling to face doubts and questions, and brain-dead: these are all public perceptions of the church as the body and thus the acting representative of Christ on earth. Honestly, it's hard to imagine being further away from the church as "a pillar and buttress of truth." Yet it remains the responsibility of pastors and Christian leaders to cast a vision for the local church that is oriented toward what the church is by divine design: a pillar and support of truth that exists to herald the light of the gospel and to "practice the truth" (1 John 1:6) before a watching world in desperate need of the good Way.

Moreover, Paul mentions in Ephesians 4:11–16 that God is specifically and strategically aiming at the intellectual maturity of individual believers as well as the church corporate. The church is, by design, to be a cradle of intellectual maturity, a place of nurture where babes in Christ grow up morally and intellectually and learn to stand on their own two feet. God graces the church with gifted individuals in order "to equip the saints for the work of ministry, for building up the body of Christ . . . to the measure of the stature of the fullness of Christ" (vv. 12–13). What is most interesting for our purposes here is that Paul takes a natural consequence of this "work of ministry," this

---

29. Kinnaman and Lyons, *UnChristian*, 123.

"building up . . . to . . . the stature of the fullness of Christ" to include and not exclude deep intellectual maturity and formation. He goes on to say that this is "so that we may no longer be children, tossed to and fro by the waves and carried about by every wind of doctrine, by human cunning, by craftiness in deceitful schemes" (v. 14). For Paul, one reason the church exists is to serve as a cradle for rearing and raising up babes in Christ to become spiritually and intellectually stable, sure-footed, and mature.

Pastors as Contemplatives, Stewards, and Guardians of the Good Deposit

I am convinced that the New Testament yields a robust, multifaceted vision of pastoral ministry that involves, among other important aims, serving as a sure-footed trail guide along the Way, leading the people of God into awe-inspiring vistas of reality and the good life and into greater depths of intellectual maturity. Carrying out this weighty task involves a dynamic interplay of "ascending" and "descending," as Gregory the Great (540–604) noted in his classic manual of Christian soul care, *The Book of Pastoral Rule.*

By Gregory's lights, pastors should be "superior to all in contemplation," and a pastor ought to excel in "raising the eyes of his heart to invisible things."[30] Pastors should regularly "ascend" to God in contemplation to be nourished and sustained by him and to refocus their mind's eye on—and realign their will to—what is ultimately true and good in Christ. It is, Gregory says, "necessary for the head to be held aloft and look forward so that the feet might go in a straight path."[31] Yet, at the same time, Gregory thinks that "true preachers do not only aspire through contemplation to the holy head of the

---

30. Gregory the Great, *Book of Pastoral Rule*, 58–59.
31. Gregory the Great, *Book of Pastoral Rule*, 70.

Church (in other words, to the Lord), but they also descend to the needs of the members through compassion." By "descending" in this way, pastors administer the grace of Christ to their people through Word and sacrament and open-handedly share the rich fruits of their contemplation with them.

When shepherds who are called to exercise "oversight" of the flock of God (see 1 Pet. 5:1–2) lay aside the contemplative life of ascent, "the laity are not able to apprehend the light of truth because, while the shepherd's mind is occupied by worldly matters, dust, driven by temptation, blinds the eyes of the Church."[32] When the overseer's vision of reality and the good life is clouded and diverted by inferior objects of sight and attention, the vision of God's people is more likely to become clouded and diverted and they run the risk of being "destroyed for lack of knowledge" (Hosea 4:6). It is for this very reason that all Christian wayfarers, and pastors in particular, are to be "contemplatives in action."[33]

Along similar lines, throughout his Pastoral Epistles Paul admonishes those in pastoral leadership to be good *stewards* and *guardians*. We normally steward and guard only what we consider to be of great value to us. The very posture of a steward and guardian denotes love, intentionality, care, watchfulness, and foresight. I was once asked to steward a bonsai tree and was assured that it would be practically impossible for it to die in my possession. The tree was dead in a week. You don't normally stumble into good and faithful stewardship; rather, it is a posture that is carefully cultivated with time and sacrifice. And we steward and guard with the greatest of sacrifice only what we value more than our own reputation, career, social media platform, and so forth.

32. Gregory the Great, *Book of Pastoral Rule*, 69.
33. This is the motto of the Jesuits, an order of Roman Catholic priests founded by Saint Ignatius of Loyola, Saint Francis Xavier, and others in 1534 for the sake of missionary endeavors. Quoted in McPherson, *Virtue and Meaning*, 175.

What are pastors supposed to be good stewards and guardians of, exactly? Pastors are, according to the apostle Paul, called to steward "the mysteries of God" (1 Cor. 4:1), which includes a particular set of ideas—namely, the "pattern of the sound words" (2 Tim. 1:13) that marks out the gospel of the Lord Jesus Christ and the broader contours of a Christian existential map. Paul considers the soul-enriching ideas contained in this deposit of sound teaching to be very precious indeed, so much so that he deems them "good" and worthy of protection, even entrusting them to Timothy (2 Tim. 1:14) and charging him to "keep a close watch on yourself and on the teaching" (1 Tim. 4:16).

Paul tells us why pastors are responsible for exercising such great care in protecting this good deposit: because it consists of "teaching that accords with godliness" (1 Tim. 6:3) and enables the saints of God to be "sound in the faith" (Titus 1:13). There is, for Paul, an organic connection between sound doctrine (literally "healthy doctrine") and sound living. And it is precisely this deep conviction that underlies Paul's urgent plea to those in pastoral ministry to be equipped and ready to "correct" (see 2 Tim. 2:25), "rebuke" (Titus 1:9), and destroy "arguments and every lofty opinion raised against the knowledge of God" (2 Cor. 10:5–6). Paul describes his own gospel ministry as aimed at the strategic dismantling of *ideological* strongholds that are contrary to the kingdom of God and taking "every thought captive to obey Christ" (2 Cor. 10:5).

So what can we conclude from our discussion of practicality questions and the distorted assumptions that tend to hide behind them? In direct contrast with the four hidden assumptions that tend to drive practicality questions, a Christian philosophical way of life is a valuable and humanly fulfilling way of being in the world *for its own sake*, is of utmost practical relevance to a well-lived human life in Christ, and can be a guiding light for pilgrims on the Way to beatitude.

CONCLUSION

Philosophy Can Change Your Life, Really

Despite my best efforts in this book, you might still find the following statement rather shocking: studying philosophy can actually change your life. Yes, you read that correctly. Surely, you might think, a dry, abstract subject like philosophy could do no such thing! My sincere hope is that, if you've traveled with me thus far, you're less inclined to think such a thing. But the philosophical assumptions that animate the workaday world are rooted very deeply within each of us and won't be uprooted by simply reading a book. Thus, I think it is appropriate to bring our journey to an end not by *telling* you that the above statement is true but by *showing* you that it is, by way of historical example. I want to conclude by peering into the life of Augustine of Hippo and exploring his two life-altering encounters with philosophy, for the purpose of casting hope that such a change is possible in your own life as well.

Many consider Augustine to be the most influential Christian mind the Western church has ever known. Indeed, it is difficult to imagine what Christendom would look like in the absence of this brilliant, heart-inflamed North African bishop. Augustine's influence on Christian thought is nearly impossible to overstate. In his *Confessions*, perhaps the liveliest and most existentially robust spiritual autobiography ever written, Augustine gives us an inside-out account of two encounters with the study of philosophy that drastically reoriented the trajectory of his young life. Let's take a look at each.

As a college freshman at the ripe young age of eighteen, Augustine began his studies at a secular university in Carthage, the once-renowned capital of Roman North Africa. Having lost his father just two years prior, Augustine tells us in vivid detail about the jagged shape of his inner life: "I came to Carthage and all around me hissed a cauldron of illicit loves . . . [and] my soul was in rotten health. In an ulcerous condition it thrust itself to outward things, miserably avid to be scratched by contact with the world of the senses."[1] Augustine's college life in Carthage was fixated on entertainment and sexual exploits and on a vain drive to intellectually dominate others.[2] A deep and abiding love for wisdom and for laying hold of the goals most worthy of human pursuit were far from the young Augustine's mind and heart at this point in his life.

As part of the university curriculum in Carthage, Augustine was assigned to read a book (now lost) titled *Hortensius*, penned by the Roman statesman and philosopher Cicero (106–43 BC), which included "an exhortation to study philosophy." In the course of reading Cicero's *Hortensius*, something shifted within the vain, illicit-desire-driven eighteen-year-old. He says exactly this in his own words: "The book changed my feelings. It altered my prayers, Lord, to be towards you yourself. It gave me different values and priorities. Suddenly every vain hope became empty to me, and I longed for the immortality of wisdom with an incredible ardour in my heart. I began to rise up

1. Augustine, *Confessions* 3.1, p. 35.
2. See Augustine, *Confessions* 3.1–3 and 3.4.7.

to return to you. . . . 'Love of wisdom' is the meaning of the Greek word *philosophia*. This book kindled my love for it."[3]

Let me encourage you to read Augustine's words again, slowly and reflectively. Augustine is giving us a first-person report of how just a few small steps on the philosophical path began to rearrange the furniture of his mind and heart and propelled him forward in the love and pursuit of wisdom. For Augustine, philosophical reflection provided the opportunity and catalyst to reorient his core *affections* ("that book changed my feelings"; "every vain hope became worthless to me"), his *highest priorities* ("it gave me different values and priorities"), and his *actions* accordingly ("I began to rise up to return to you"): a total life reorientation, you might say.

Here again we have the dynamic interplay between the mind, the will, and action. Augustine was awakened to wonder about a reality much bigger than himself and to pursuits that were much more satisfying and enduring than the fleeting pleasures of his former ways. While this existential reorientation aided by philosophy would fall well short of a total, spiritual transformation at this point in Augustine's journey (there would be many stumbles and falls along his way to the cross of Christ), it nevertheless was a definitive turning point that would forever alter the trajectory of his life. Philosopher James K. A. Smith insightfully comments on this kind of existential reorientation that can be jump-started by philosophical reflection:

> In a university that revolves around the quest for profit and prestige, a lingering liberal arts curriculum is like a distant echo that keeps calling. You never know when the still, small voice of Plato can pierce through all the noise in a marauding frat boy's life and resound as a wake-up call for a soul—that his taut, frantic, voracious body *has* a soul, that the soul is made for a quest and not just sexual conquests,

3. Augustine, *Confessions* 3.4, p. 39.

and that there is a kind of learning that doesn't just position you but transforms you.[4]

For Augustine, whose life at that time hinged on the satisfaction of disordered loves and whose eyes were enthralled by false visions of the good life, the study of philosophy couldn't have been more practical, in the best sense of the word.

This wouldn't be the only time philosophical reflection would serve as the catalyst for reorienting the center of gravity of Augustine's mind and heart. Later in his life, as a thirty-one-year-old living in Milan, Italy (June–July 386), Augustine found himself in the intellectual grip of a materialist metaphysic, a one-dimensional view of reality that confined reality to what is made up of matter or is extended in space. He says, "I had no clear vision even of my own self. I thought simply non-existent anything not extended in space or diffused or concentrated or expanding, which does not possess, or is incapable of possessing, such qualities."[5]

It was after studying "the books of the Platonists" (likely Proclus and Porphyry) that he began to seriously consider new intellectual possibilities—in particular, that reality just might consist of more than meets the eye.[6] It was a Platonic understanding of reality, in particular the existence of an unchanging, immaterial realm, that provided a new intellectual scaffolding that made the Christian story a live, intellectual option for Augustine. He confesses to God, "At that time, after reading the books of the Platonists and learning from them to seek for immaterial truth, I turned my attention to your 'invisible nature understood through the things which are made (Rom. 1:20).'"[7]

4. J. K. A. Smith, *On the Road with St. Augustine*, 143.
5. Augustine, *Confessions* 7.2, p. 112.
6. Augustine, *Confessions* 7.13, p. 121.
7. Augustine, *Confessions* 7.26, pp. 129–30.

While Augustine quickly recognized that Platonism fell well short of the full-blooded Christian gospel of "the Word become flesh," it certainly helped liberate him from the confined, one-dimensional view of reality that had once held his imagination captive. In God's providence, Augustine later recognized that his philosophical study had helped till the soil of his mind to be intellectually open and receptive to the gospel in all its fullness in Christ, a gospel that was not found in the books of the Platonists: "I believe that you wanted me to encounter them [Platonists] before I came to study your scriptures."[8]

Not once but twice the study of philosophy changed Augustine's life. And there's no reason it can't change yours too. So I leave you, dear reader, with one final question: What are *you* waiting for?

8. Augustine, *Confessions* 7.26, p. 130.

BIBLIOGRAPHY

Adams, Marilyn McCord. "*Fides quaerens intellectum*: Anselm's Method in Philosophical Theology." *Faith and Philosophy* 9, no. 4 (1992): 409–35.

Allen, Michael. *Grounded in Heaven: Recentering Christian Hope and Life on God.* Grand Rapids: Eerdmans, 2018.

Allen, Summer. "The Science of Awe." *Greater Good Science Center*, September 2018, 1–45.

Anselm. *Anselm: Basic Writings.* Translated by Thomas Williams. Indianapolis: Hackett, 2007.

Aristotle. *A New Aristotle Reader.* Edited by J. L. Ackrill. Princeton: Princeton University Press, 1987.

———. *Nicomachean Ethics.* 3rd ed. Translated by Terrence Irwin. Indianapolis: Hackett, 2019.

Augustine. *Confessions.* Translated by Henry Chadwick. New York: Oxford University Press, 2008.

———. *Sermons 51–94.* Translated by Edmund Hill. The Works of Saint Augustine III/3. New York: New City, 1991.

———. *St. Augustine's City of God and Christian Doctrine.* Edited by Philip Schaff. Translated by J. F. Shaw. A Select Library of the Nicene and Post-Nicene Fathers of the Christian Church, series 1, vol. 2. Buffalo: Christian Literature Company, 1887.

———. *The Trinity*. Edited by Hermigild Dressler. Translated by Stephen McKenna. The Fathers of the Church 45. Washington, DC: Catholic University of America Press, 1963.

Bai, Yang, Laura A. Maruskin, Serena Chen, Amie M. Gordon, Jennifer E. Stellar, Galen D. McNeil, Kaiping Peng, and Dacher Keltner. "Awe, the Diminished Self, and Collective Engagement: Universals and Cultural Variations in the Small Self." *Journal of Personality and Social Psychology* 113, no. 2 (2017): 185–209.

Bauerschmidt, Fredrick Christian. *Thomas Aquinas: Faith, Reason, and Following Christ*. Oxford: Oxford University Press, 2013.

Bilbro, Jeffrey. *Reading the Times: A Literary and Theological Inquiry into the News*. Downers Grove, IL: InterVarsity, 2021.

Boersma, Hans. *Seeing God: The Beatific Vision in the Christian Tradition*. Grand Rapids: Eerdmans, 2018.

Boethius. *The Consolation of Philosophy*. Translated by Victor Watts. London: Penguin, 1999.

Burt, Donald X. *Friendship and Society: An Introduction to Augustine's Practical Philosophy*. Grand Rapids: Eerdmans, 1999.

Caldecott, Stratford. *Beauty for Truth's Sake: On the Re-enchantment of Education*. Grand Rapids: Brazos, 2009.

Calvin, John. *Institutes of the Christian Religion*. Edited by John T. McNeill. Translated by Ford Lewis Battles. Louisville: Westminster John Knox, 1960.

Chan, Simon. *Spiritual Theology: A Systematic Study of the Christian Life*. Downers Grove, IL: InterVarsity, 1998.

Cicero. *On Old Age, on Friendship, on Divination*. Translated by W. A. Falconer. Loeb Classical Library 154. Cambridge, MA: Harvard University Press, 1923.

Cohoe, Caleb M., and Stephen R. Grimm. "What It Takes to Live Philosophically: Or, How to Progress in the Art of Living." In *Philosophy as a Way of Life: Historical, Contemporary, and Pedagogical Perspectives*, edited by James M. Ambury, Tushar Irani, and Kathleen Wallace, 229–48. Malden, MA: Wiley & Sons, 2021.

Cooper, John. "Ancient Philosophy as a Way of Life." Lecture delivered at the Tanner Lectures on Human Values, Stanford University, January 25–26, 2012.

———. *Pursuits of Wisdom: Six Ways of Life in Ancient Philosophy from Socrates to Plotinus*. Princeton: Princeton University Press, 2013.

Crawford, Matthew. *The World beyond Your Head: On Becoming an Individual in an Age of Distraction*. New York: Farrar, Straus & Giroux, 2015.

Cyr, Taylor, and Philip Swenson. "Learning in the Time of the Pandemic." *Psychology Today*, March 25, 2020. https://www.psychologytoday.com/us/blog/moral-talk/202003/learning-in-the-time-the-pandemic.

Daley, Brian. *Gregory of Nazianzus*. London: Routledge, 2006.

Dante Alighieri. *Inferno*. Translated by Anthony Esolen. New York: Random House, 2003.

Descartes, René. *Discourse on Method*. 4th ed. Translated by Donald A. Cress. Indianapolis: Hackett, 1998.

Deweese, Garrett J. *Doing Philosophy as a Christian*. Downers Grove, IL: InterVarsity, 2011.

DeYoung, Rebecca Konyndyk. *Glittering Vices: A New Look at the Seven Deadly Sins and Their Remedies*. 2nd ed. Grand Rapids: Brazos, 2020.

Foster, Richard J., and Emilie Griffin, eds. *Spiritual Classics*. New York: HarperCollins, 2000.

Frede, Michael. *Essays in Ancient Philosophy*. Minneapolis: University of Minnesota Press, 1987.

Galen. *Galen: Selected Works*. Translated by Peter N. Singer. Oxford: Oxford University Press, 1997.

Ganssle, Gregory E. *Our Deepest Desires*. Downers Grove, IL: InterVarsity, 2017.

Gregory Nazianzen. "Select Orations of Saint Gregory Nazianzen." In *S. Cyril of Jerusalem, S. Gregory Nazianzen*, edited by Philip Schaff and

Henry Wace, 402–22. Translated by Charles Gordon Browne and James Edward Swallow. A Select Library of the Nicene and Post-Nicene Fathers of the Christian Church, series 2, vol. 7. New York: Christian Literature Company, 1894.

Gregory of Nyssa. *Gregory of Nyssa: Dogmatic Treatises, Etc.* Edited by Philip Schaff and Henry Wace. Translated by William Moore. A Select Library of the Nicene and Post-Nicene Fathers of the Christian Church, series 2, vol. 5. New York: Christian Literature Company, 1893.

———. *Homilies on the Song of Songs.* Translated by Richard A. Norris Jr. Atlanta: Society of Biblical Literature, 2012.

Gregory the Great. *The Book of Pastoral Rule.* Translated by George E. Demacopoulos. New York: St. Vladimir's Seminary Press, 2007.

Grimm, Stephen R., and Caleb M. Cohoe. "What Is Philosophy as a Way of Life? *Why* Philosophy as a Way of Life?" *European Journal of Philosophy* 21 (2021): 236–51.

Hadot, Pierre. *Philosophy as a Way of Life.* Malden, MA: Blackwell, 1995.

———. *What Is Ancient Philosophy?* Cambridge, MA: Harvard University Press, 2002.

Harari, Yuval Noah. *Homo Deus: A Brief History of Tomorrow.* New York: HarperCollins, 2017.

Harkins, Franklin T. "Introduction to *Didascalicon on the Study of Reading.*" In *Interpretation of Scripture: Theory; A Selection of Works of Hugh, Andrew, Richard and Godfrey of St. Victor, and of Robert of Melun*, edited by Franklin T. Harkins and Frans van Liere, 64–79. New York: New City, 2013.

Hitz, Zena. *Lost in Thought: The Hidden Pleasures of an Intellectual Life.* Princeton: Princeton University Press, 2020.

Hugh of Saint Victor. *Didascalicon on the Study of Reading.*" In *Interpretation of Scripture: Theory; A Selection of Works of Hugh, Andrew, Richard and Godfrey of St. Victor, and of Robert of Melun*, edited by Franklin T. Harkins and Frans van Liere, 61–202. New York: New City, 2013.

Hutter, Reinhard. *Bound for Beatitude: A Thomistic Study in Eschatology and Ethics*. Washington, DC: Catholic University of America Press, 2019.

Ignatius. *The Spiritual Exercises of St. Ignatius*. Translated by Louis J. Puhl. Chicago: Loyola University Press, 1951.

Inman, Ross. "Epistemic Temperance and the Moral Perils of Intellectual Inquiry." *Philosophia Christi* 17, no. 2 (2015): 457–72.

Irenaeus. *The Apostolic Fathers with Justin Martyr and Irenaeus*. Edited by Alexander Roberts, James Donaldson, and A. Cleveland Coxe. Ante-Nicene Fathers 1. Buffalo: Christian Literature Company, 1885.

Jamieson, R. B., and Tyler R. Wittman. *Biblical Reasoning: Christological and Trinitarian Rules for Exegesis*. Grand Rapids: Baker Academic, 2022.

John Paul II. "Fides et ratio." The Holy See, September 20, 2022. https://www.vatican.va/content/john-paul-ii/en/encyclicals/documents/hf_jp-ii_enc_14091998_fides-et-ratio.html.

Keltner, Dacher, and Jonathan Haidt. "Approaching Awe, a Moral, Spiritual, and Aesthetic Emotion." *Cognition and Emotion* 17, no. 2 (2003): 297–314.

King, Nathan. *The Excellent Mind: Intellectual Virtues for Everyday Life*. New York: Oxford University Press, 2021.

Kinnaman, David, and Gabe Lyons. *UnChristian: What a New Generation Really Thinks about Christianity . . . and Why It Matters*. Grand Rapids: Baker Books, 2007.

Lane, Anthony N. S. *John Calvin: Student of the Church Fathers*. Grand Rapids: Baker Academic, 2000.

Lewis, C. S. *The Discarded Image*. Cambridge: Cambridge University Press, 1964.

———. *The Four Loves*. New York: Harcourt, Brace & World, 1960.

———. *Mere Christianity*. New York: HarperCollins, 2001.

Mashek, Debra, Lisa W. Cannaday, and June P. Tangney. "Inclusion of Community in Self Scale: A Single-Item Pictorial Measure of Community Connectedness." *Journal of Community Psychology* 35, no. 2 (2007): 257–75.

McBrayer, Justin P. *Beyond Fake News: Finding the Truth in a World of Misinformation*. New York: Routledge, 2021.

McKirland, Christa L. *God's Provision, Humanity's Need: The Gift of Our Dependence.* Grand Rapids: Baker Academic, 2022.

McPherson, David. *Virtue and Meaning: A Neo-Aristotelian Perspective.* New York: Cambridge University Press, 2020.

———. *The Virtues of Limits.* Oxford: Oxford University Press, 2022.

Midgley, Mary. *What Is Philosophy For?* London: Bloomsbury Academic, 2018.

Morris, Tom. *Philosophy for Dummies.* Foster City, CA: IDG Books, 1999.

Newbigin, Lesslie. *Foolishness to the Greeks: The Gospel and Western Culture.* Grand Rapids: Eerdmans, 1986.

Nguyen, C. Thi. "Escape the Echo Chamber." *Aeon*, April 9, 2018. https://aeon.co/essays/why-its-as-hard-to-escape-an-echo-chamber-as-it-is-to-flee-a-cult.

Nouwen, Henri. *The Way of the Heart: Desert Spirituality and Contemporary Ministry.* San Francisco: HarperSanFrancisco, 1991.

Nussbaum, Martha C. *Therapy of Desire: Theory and Practice in Hellenistic Ethics.* Princeton: Princeton University Press, 1994.

Odell, Jenny. *How to Do Nothing: Resisting the Attention Economy.* Brooklyn, NY: Melville House, 2019.

Paquette, Jonah. *Awestruck: How Embracing Wonder Can Make You Happier, Healthier, and More Connected.* Boulder, CO: Shambhala, 2020.

Perlin, Joshua D., and Leon Li. "Why Does Awe Have Prosocial Effects? New Perspectives on Awe and the Small Self." *Perspectives on Psychological Science* 15, no. 2 (2020): 291–308.

Philips, Philip Edward. "Lady Philosophy's Therapeutic Method: The 'Gentler' and 'Stronger' Remedies in Boethius's *De consolatione philosophiae*." *Medieval English Studies* 10, no. 2 (2002): 5–26.

Pieper, Josef. *For the Love of Wisdom: Essays on the Nature of Philosophy.* San Francisco: Ignatius, 2006.

———. *Happiness and Contemplation.* South Bend, IN: St. Augustine's Press, 1998.

———. *In Defense of Philosophy.* San Francisco: Ignatius, 1992.

———. *Josef Pieper: An Anthology*. San Francisco: Ignatius, 1989.

———. *Leisure: The Basis of Culture*. San Francisco: Ignatius, 2009.

———. *Only the Lover Sings: Art and Contemplation*. San Francisco: Ignatius, 1990.

———. *The Philosophical Act*. San Francisco: Ignatius, 2009.

Plantinga, Cornelius, Jr. *Not the Way It's Supposed to Be: A Breviary of Sin*. Grand Rapids: Eerdmans, 1995.

Plato. *Plato: Complete Works*. Edited by John Cooper. Indianapolis: Hackett, 1997.

———. *The Trial and Death of Socrates*. 3rd ed. Translated by G. M. A. Grube. Indianapolis: Hackett, 2000.

Plutarch. *Moralia*. Edited by Frank Cole Babbitt. Medford, MA: Harvard University Press, 1928.

Postman, Neil. *Amusing Ourselves to Death: Public Discourse in the Age of Show Business*. New York: Penguin Group, 2006.

Reinke, Tony. *Competing Spectacles: Treasuring Christ in the Media Age*. Wheaton: Crossway, 2019.

Richard. *The Mystical Ark*. Translated by Grover A. Zinn. New York: Paulist Press, 1979.

Rievaulx, Aelred. *Spiritual Friendship*. Translated by Lawrence C. Braceland. Trappist, KY: Cistercian Publications, 2010.

Rosa, Hartmut. *The Uncontrollability of the World*. Medford, MA: Polity, 2020.

Sacks, Jonathan. *The Great Partnership: God, Science and the Search for Meaning*. London: Hodder & Stoughton, 2011.

Saucy, Robert. *Minding the Heart: The Way of Spiritual Transformation*. Grand Rapids: Kregel, 2013.

Schmid, Wolfgang. "Boethius and the Claims of Philosophy." *Studia Patristica* 2 (1957): 368–75.

Schwartz, Daniel. *Aquinas on Friendship*. Oxford: Oxford University Press, 2007.

Sharpe, Matthew, and Michael Ure. *Philosophy as a Way of Life: History, Dimensions, Directions*. London: Bloomsbury Academic, 2021.

Smith, James K. A. *On the Road with St. Augustine: A Real-World Spirituality for Restless Hearts*. Grand Rapids: Brazos, 2019.

Smith, Randall. "'If Philosophy Begins in Wonder': Aquinas, Creation, and Wonder." *Communio: International Catholic Review* 41 (Spring 2014): 92–111.

Stellar, Jennifer E., Amie Gordon, Craig L. Anderson, Paul K. Piff, Galen D. McNeil, and Dacher Keltner. "Awe and Humility." *Journal of Personality and Social Psychology* 114, no. 2 (2018): 258–69.

Taylor, Charles. *The Malaise of Modernity*. Toronto: Anansi, 1991.

———. *A Secular Age*. Cambridge, MA: Harvard University Press, 2007.

Ten Elshof, Gregg. *I Told Me So: Self-Deception and the Christian Life*. Grand Rapids: Eerdmans, 2009.

Thomas Aquinas. *Commentary on the Metaphysics of Aristotle*. Translated by John P. Rowan. Chicago: Henry Regnery, 1961.

———. *Summa contra Gentiles*. Translated by Vernon J. Bourke. 4 vols. Notre Dame, IN: University of Notre Dame Press, 1975.

———. *Summa theologiae*. Translated by Laurence Shapcote. Lander, WY: Aquinas Institute, 2012.

———. *Thomas Aquinas: Selected Writings*. Translated by Ralph McInerny. London: Penguin Books, 1998.

Trueman, Carl R. *The Rise and Triumph of the Modern Self*. Wheaton: Crossway, 2020.

———. *Strange New World: How Thinkers and Activists Redefined Identity and Sparked the Sexual Revolution*. Wheaton: Crossway, 2022.

Valdesolo, Piercarlo, Andrew Shtulman, and Andrew S. Baron. "Science Is Awe-Some: The Emotional Antecedents of Science Learning." *Emotion Review* 9, no. 3 (2017): 215–21.

Vanhoozer, Kevin. *Hearers and Doers: A Pastor's Guide to Making Disciples through Scripture and Doctrine*. Bellingham, WA: Lexham, 2019.

Vanhoozer, Kevin, and Owen Strachan. *The Pastor as Public Theologian: Reclaiming a Lost Vision*. Grand Rapids: Baker Academic, 2015.

Van Nieuwenhove, Rik. *Thomas Aquinas and Contemplation*. Oxford: Oxford University Press, 2021.

Webster, John. *Domain of the Word: Scripture and Theological Reason.* New York: Bloomsbury T&T Clark, 2013.

Whitehead, Alfred N. "Remarks." *Philosophical Review* 46 (1937): 178–86.

Willard, Dallas. *Knowing Christ Today: Why We Can Trust Spiritual Knowledge.* New York: HarperCollins, 2009.

———. *Renewing the Christian Mind.* New York: HarperCollins, 2016.

———. *The Spirit of the Disciplines: Understanding How God Changes Lives.* New York: HarperCollins, 1988.

Yaden, David B., Jonathan Iwry, Kelley J. Slack, Johannes C. Eiechstaedt, Yukun Zhao, George E. Vaillant, and Andrew B. Newberg. "The Overview Effect: Awe and Self-Transcendent Experience in Space Flight." *Psychology of Consciousness: Theory, Research, and Practice* 3, no. 1 (2016): 1–11.

SCRIPTURE INDEX

SUBJECT INDEX